LOSING TO WIN

IRENE BUCHANAN
31 The Hill, Thornhill, Stirling FK8 3PT Scotland

D1438116

LOSING TO WIN

How Loss Can Mean Gain

Bill Hybels
and *Rob Wilkins*

Marshall Pickering
An Imprint of HarperCollins*Publishers*

Marshall Pickering is an Imprint of
HarperCollins*Religious*
Part of HarperCollins*Publishers*
77–85 Fulham Palace Road,
Hammersmith, London W6 8JB

First published in the United States of America by
Zondervan Publishing House in 1993 as *Descending Into Greatness*

This edition first published in Great Britain
in 1993 by Marshall Pickering
1 3 5 7 9 10 8 6 4 2

Copyright © 1993 Bill Hybels

Bill Hybels asserts the moral right to
be identified as the author of this work

A catalogue record for this book
is available from the British Library

ISBN 0 551 02807 6

Printed in Great Britain by
HarperCollinsManufacturing Glasgow

CONDITIONS OF SALE

All rights reserved. No part of this publication may be
reproduced, stored in a retrieval system, or transmitted,
in any form or by any means, electronic, mechanical,
photocopying, recording or otherwise, without the prior
permission of the publishers.

This book is sold subject to the condition that it shall not,
by way of trade or otherwise, be lent, re-sold, hired out or
otherwise circulated without the publisher's prior consent
in any form of binding or cover other than that in which it
is published and without a similar condition including this
condition being imposed on the subsequent purchaser.

All Scripture quotations, unless indicated, are taken from the
Holy Bible, New International Version®. NIV®. Copyright © 1973,
1978, 1984 by International Bible Society. Used by permission of
Hodder & Stoughton. All rights reserved.

Verses marked KJV are from the King James Version of the Bible.

To Dr. Gilbert Bilezikian,
whose life has been a nonstop testament
to what this book is about.

Thanks Gil . . .
You started teaching me these lessons
twenty years ago, and you're finding new ways
to teach them all the time.

Contents

PREFACE

*R*ob Wilkins is an extraordinary writer. Beyond that, he is an extraordinary person—a man of sensitivity, passion, and keen thought. Though we are "wired up" about as differently as two humans can be—in temperament and giftedness—we were both seized by the importance of the subject matter of this book and captivated by the possibility of working together.

The marriage of our gifts which this book required was not an easy one. I am a teacher; Rob is a journalist. I am a pragmatist; Rob is an artist. I like to get where I'm going as directly as possible; Rob prefers the scenic route. I wanted to make a forceful presentation of the biblical case for "descending." Rob wanted to put twentieth century skin on the biblical lessons. We decided to do both, to teach and then flesh out the teaching in contemporary illustrations.

Rob took arm loads of my messages, outlines, and taped interviews, then sequestered himself long enough to let the scriptural concept of downward mobility bleed onto the pages of this book. Then he immersed himself in the lives of a handful of people who are attempting to do more than just read about descending into greatness. I am deeply indebted to Rob and his wife, Melanie, for their enormous investment in this book.

Once again my wife, Lynne, who plays a key role in virtually everything I write, deserves a sincere thank you for serving as the final editor.

Our friends at Zondervan continue to make our publishing feel more like team ministry than simply the book business.

My prayer, and the prayer of each person who contributed to this book, is that *Descending Into Greatness* will become, for every reader, a lifestyle that leads to joy.

ACKNOWLEDGMENTS

As I read through the final proofs of this book, I was, once again, gripped by the *scriptural challenge* of downward mobility. Since my conversion to Christianity at age sixteen, I have gained great respect for the power of the Word of God—the two-edged sword that has, time and again, painfully cut away the diseased portions of my heart and pierced my soul with healing.

But also as I read, I was gripped by the *real life challenges* offered by the people whose lives are profiled in this book. Their stories posed questions that I found difficult to answer. For example:

If I faced the clash of values that Lance Murdock faces every day, would I have the discipline and purity of heart to hang on to Truth?

If my commitment to God called me to haul my family across continents and cultures, would I be willing to do it, as Dr. Jim Judge did?

If asked to serve for decades in a dusty land scattered with forgotten people, would I respond with the servant's heart that beats in Angie Garber?

If I lived the life of Mike Singletary, would I, like him, be called a humble man?

If called to be "obedient unto death," would I leave a legacy of loving as Lorrie Shaver did?

11

If dealt the blows life dealt John and Gwenn Tindall, would I have their courage to crawl through the brokenness until I found joy?

I wholeheartedly thank these people for allowing their stories to be included in this book, and for allowing their lives to challenge mine.

DESCENDING

1

THE PATH
TO GREATNESS

"Your attitude should be the same as that of Christ Jesus."

—*Philippians 2:5*

*I*n the vocabulary of the world, "down" is a word reserved for losers, cowards, and the bear market. It is a word to be avoided or ignored, and certainly not discussed seriously, especially in polite society. It is a word that colors whatever it touches, even the otherwise proper company of words that it keeps: down and out, downfall, downscale, downhill, downhearted and, worst of all, down under. A word, it seems, only on the unfortunate lips of the weak, the poor, or the dead.

If all that weren't enough, there is this crowning blow against the word: Its antonym is "up." And up, in our high-voltage society, is a word that has come to be cherished, almost worshiped. It is a word reserved for the winners, heroes, and those who know their bull. It is a word to be admired and pursued, the unspoken talk of the party, the way to influence whoever is present: upscale, up and coming, upwardly mobile, upper class. The word of the chosen few and the strong.

Although the decade of the eighties soiled the purity of the word with a lingering aftertaste of greed, up still carries a strong appeal. It exudes a sense of virility and health, of well-being, of feeling . . . well . . . up. You *rise* against gravity, the odds, the crowd, or whatever happens to get in the way. You *ascend* to fame, money, spotlights, power, comfort, and pleasure. Up, clearly, is the direction of greatness.

From the world's perspective, it is the only direction to go. Just as a compass needle points north, the human needle points up; in each heart is a built-in mechanism that craves self-promotion and advancement, the climb of ego. Our role models and heroes reinforce the theme: Ascend and flex the muscles of your self-will. Do whatever it takes to conquer gravity. Whether you do it blatantly or wear the disguise of humility, make yourself upwardly mobile. Why? Because that is the direction of greatness.

That is what the world says. In such a context, Philippians 2 may be the most countercultural chapter in the Bible, especially for trendsetting, young professionals. Simply stated, the message of Philippians is this: If you want to be truly great, then the direction you must go is down. You must descend into greatness. At the heart of this paradox is still another paradox:

Greatness is not a measure of self-will, but rather self-abandonment. The more you lose, the more you gain.

On the surface, one can understand the world's reservations. Descending into greatness seems absurd, a classical oxymoron. In fact, Philippians makes it clear that descending is everything the world cracks it up to be: demotion, anonymity, servanthood, downscaling, decreasing, losing, and dying. Even the best Manhattan advertising agencies would be hard pressed for a catchy jingle. *Lose it all. Imagine the possibilities.*

The world is not alone in its unwillingness to buy into the idea of descending. Throughout history, few Christians have really come to grips with the concept of downward mobility. Many of today's Christians confuse their faith with a wish list for self-indulgence instead of a renunciation of selfish desires. How many Christians do you know who have recently downscaled or decreased or given sacrificially so the cause of Christ might be advanced? Let's make the question even more specific: What about you? Do you really believe that losing your life is the way to gain it?

Difficult as the concept is to act on, Philippians makes it clear that moving down is the *only* way to become great in God's eyes. Downward mobility is not simply the best of many optional paths a Christian can take to bring God pleasure. It is the only path.

DESCENDING WITH A TWIST

Although the idea of descending into greatness seems to be inherently illogical at first glance, the depth and beauty of its wisdom reveal itself upon closer examination.

The first and certainly greatest reason for believing in the power of downward mobility is the example of Christ. Philippians 2 tells us that Jesus stooped to love. He bent over backward to concern Himself with others' needs. Such a descent seems like an illogical way for the Son of God to try to impact the world. Yet even the most defiant unbeliever has a difficult time denying Christ's impact; not just any man steps into history and splits time in two. From the world's point of view, many things about Christ can be debated: His sanity, His honesty, His motivation. But there is no question that He left on history the mark of a great man.

But Christ's path to greatness was not a typical one. The Bible makes it clear that He came "down" into the world—and He came down from the very top. Philippians 2 states that Christ was "equal with God." He was the ultimate object of praise in the universe He had created. Given His high position, the violence of the incarnation and the depth of Jesus' descent takes on astonishing dimensions. He voluntarily sacrificed His divine prerogatives. The One worthy of all worship and the Source of all power was born as a helpless baby in a dirty animal stable.

Once His life on earth began, Jesus never stopped descending. Omnipotent, He cried; the owner of all things, He had no home. The King of Kings, He became a bondservant; the source of truth, He was found guilty of blasphemy; the Creator, He was spit on by the creatures; the giver of life, He was crucified naked on a cross—bleeding, gasping for air. With His death, the descent was complete—from the pinnacle of praise in the universe to the ultimate debasement and torture of death on a cross, the innocent victim of human wickedness.

With His life and death as a man, Christ violated every tenet of the world's system. The Highest came to serve the lowest. The Creator and Sustainer of all things came to pour Himself out. The One who possessed everything became nothing. From the world's perspective, the cross became the symbol of foolishness. Yet in God's eyes, Christ became the greatest of the great. He had accomplished totally the purpose for which God had sent Him; He had pleased His Father and advanced God's kingdom on earth. And Philippians states that because of Christ's downward mobility, God highly exalted Him, and gave Him a name above every name. That's the twist. Jesus Christ descended into God's greatness.

DEMONSTRATING LOVE

Much was required of Jesus Christ. God asked Him to give up everything, to descend into humiliation, pain, and finally, death on a cross. It would be easy to think, if we let our minds get careless, that God was not a very loving father. How could a father ask his only son to endure torture, beatings, and unfathomable suffering? How can love manifest itself in such a seemingly brutal fashion? The answer must be that God so loved the world. Jesus Christ suffered for righteousness sake, *as* God and *for* God. It was the highest possible demonstration of God's love.

Hebrews 12:2 is one of the most stunning and provocative verses in the Bible: "Let us fix our eyes on Jesus, the author and perfecter of our faith, who for the joy set before him endured the cross, scorning its shame, and sat down at the right hand of the throne of God." Jesus endured for the joy of accomplishing the purpose of God, namely to demonstrate His love and accept the penalty for your sin and mine. He came to bleed, for each of us.

There was another reason for Christ's downward mobility: to model for His followers what it meant to demonstrate the love of God. The passage in Philippians describing Christ's descent begins with these words: "Let this mind be in you, which was also in Christ Jesus" (Philippians 2:5, KJV). In other words, "Read the words that follow carefully; they're meant for you too." Just as Jesus made Himself downwardly mobile and gave Himself away for the benefit of others, we are expected to do the same, even to the point of suffering and death, if need be.

It's not that God has a problem with seeing His children in places of honor and glory. In truth, He longs to exalt them. What concerns Him is upward mobility as defined by the world: to promote ourselves, to advance our own cause, to push our own agenda at the expense of others. The end goal is to arrive at the top of the heap with enough money, power, and material possessions to feed one's main objective: self-indulgence. That's why God has a problem with the world's approach to greatness. He knows that self-indulgence, by its very nature, always leads to self-destruction. What seems like a climb to the top, to a deep sense of self-fulfillment, turns out to be the digging of one's own grave. Up, in God's dictionary, always leads down.

And down leads up. James 4:10 says, "Humble yourselves before the Lord, and he will lift you up."

Jesus Christ descended, decreased, and downscaled so that He might perfectly demonstrate the love of God. He made Himself nothing in order to accomplish the purposes of His Father. And God, in turn, highly exalted Him.

DESCENDING INTO GREATNESS

Down is a word for losers. That is what Philippians 2 says. God is calling on Christians to develop the discipline of losing. *If you want to follow me,* God says, *follow the example of My Son, who lost not just a little, nor even a lot, but lost everything.*

Such a call does not paint a picture of men and women drained and empty, devoid of personality and energy. God's call to lose for His sake doesn't mean we deny the legitimate needs of our human frame or the desires and passions He has placed within us. Jesus took care of Himself physically and emotionally, and He challenged His followers to embrace their uniqueness and pursue the dreams God had given them. But losing does mean that we allow God to determine what needs are legitimate. Losing means to yield our desires and passions to His guidance; to invite Him to chip away the rough edges of our personalities; to use our gifts without seeking applause; and to allow Him to conform our dreams to His will.

Such losing is not easy. It requires a singular focus on Jesus Christ, an unwavering passion and love for God and the advancement of His kingdom, and the development and consistent exercise of spiritual disciplines. The faint of heart need not apply.

Yet God asks us to lose so we can gain. He makes a hard request, then offers a promise. *Lose your selfish ambition; I will honor you for loving others. Lose your addiction to things; I will provide for you if you seek Me wholeheartedly. Lose your obsession to be in control; I will give you power as you follow Me. Lose your appetite for thrills; I will startle you with pleasures you could never have found on your own. Lose your life; I will give you eternity.*

It is a seemingly brutal path love often takes: a life of losing, of self-demotion, even dying. But the Bible is stubbornly insistent about this: It is, at the same time, the path that leads to joy.

If you are like me, you will not find *Descending into Greatness* ranking as the easiest or most pleasant book on your shelf to read. I can think of no other study in the Bible that has disturbed and unsettled me more. The joy comes—yes—but often not without some pain first. Philippians 2 carries a mean punch.

Yet those of us who truly want to be devoted followers of Jesus Christ must learn the lessons of Philippians 2. Few other passages communicate more clearly who Jesus is, and therefore, who we are called to be. It is through submitting to the challenge of this passage that we can learn the day-by-day discipline of descending into God's greatness—which is the highest calling in life.

POWER

2

THE TWO
KINGS

> "Who, being in very nature God, did not consider
> equality with God something to be grasped."
> —Philippians 2:6

Power.

Standing by itself, there is an edge to the word.
We are not sure how to react: to desire or to cringe.

But we know what the word means. We understand what it is to stand on its two sides: consumed in
its energy, wasted by its blind fury. Power, simply defined, is the ability to control resources to secure one's
own destiny. Kings and slaves, wars and treaties, colo-
nies and nations, coups and elections all share the common denominator of power. Through the centuries,
from the time of the Fall, it has been the single greatest
catalyst of history. Adler described it as the great human obsession. Kissinger referred to it as an aphrodi-

siac. The apostle Paul linked it, more times than not, to something he called sin.

Much has been written about power. Its message is everywhere—in history books, psychology texts, religious creeds, graffiti, physics manuals, marriage certificates, the *New York Times*. But of the endless number of pages written about power, none seems to me more striking, disturbing, or puzzling than the second chapter of the book of Matthew.

It is essentially the story of two kings.

One is named Herod. The other is Jesus Christ. In all of history, perhaps, never were two men more opposite. Their rightful claim to kingship was nearly all they shared. The contrast, however, is most striking when it comes to how they managed power.

OBSESSED WITH UP

The story began on the edge of absurdity. Herod the Great, the king of Judea, a person not known for his humility, was concerned when he heard rumor that a baby had been born who some said would grow up to be King of the Jews. If there was one thing Herod hated, it was potential rivals—even if the rival was a helpless baby in a stable. And he would do anything to defeat a rival, anything to avoid losing his grip on power. At first Herod used deception, a favorite technique, to try to discover the location of the prophesied king. When that didn't work, he ordered the execution of all boys under the age of two in Bethlehem and the surrounding area. With one order from Herod, many innocent children died.

As outrageous as that act was, it came as no surprise. King Herod had a track record. He was more than crazy—He was addicted to power and made mad by it. When you blow the dust off a history book and unravel the mysteries of the political situation in Palestine at that time, Herod emerges larger than life and death. Born into a politically well-connected family in 73 B.C., Herod was destined for a life of hardball and power brokering. Talk around his dining room table centered around how to undermine a political opponent and how to defend against betrayal and backstabbing. Power was all that mattered. Herod, on a superficial level, seemed built for it. By stature, he was tall and imposing; by personality, competitive and cruel.

For Herod, power meant movement. And the direction, in every single case, was *up.* In fact, these two letters could easily serve as a masthead or a tombstone inscription as to what Herod was all about as a person. Rarely has history recorded so clearly the life of someone so obsessed with moving up.

To make matters worse, his obsession with power was tinged with a passion for revenge. His father, also a king, was poisoned by a political opponent. Something snapped inside of Herod when he saw firsthand how vulnerable political rulers could be. It was a turning point in his life. Seething with the desire for revenge, Herod formed an ingenious plan: he invited his father's killers over for a dinner party. His greeters just happened to be hit men. Herod, according to the history books, slept well that night. He was never particularly vulnerable to remorse.

From that point on, Herod made the calculated decision to never expose himself to the possibility of a secret ingredient winding up in *his* soup. His life revolved around covering all his power bases, and he thought nothing of using brute force to do so. He frequently barked out orders that resulted in arrests, beatings, extortion, blackmail, kidnappings, torture, and execution. In fact, the intensity of his violence grew in direct proportion to the amount of power he possessed.

But brute force was just one of his tactics; his strategies were multifaceted. If necessity called for a more diplomatic approach, he was calculating enough to present a softer, kinder image. He knew and practiced the art of gentle stroking and employed the secrets of ingratiation. He engineered a food and clothing distribution system during a time of famine; he identified and bankrolled construction projects to excite certain special-interest groups (including remodeling the Jewish temple in downtown Jerusalem). In reality, Herod had little or no interest in the poor or the special-interest groups. He was, however, smart enough to know that loyalty could be bought. He served himself by serving others.

The idea was to make an impression. He arranged relationships to be conduits for power. Herod built a city and a state-of-the-art harbor along the Mediterranean coast. It was, perhaps, one of his more successful stabs at self-promotion. It increased trade in his domain, and he earned favor with his boss by naming the city after him. Caesarea. Herod knew that obtaining power meant getting close to its sources. And speaking of kissing up, several of Herod's ten marriages were politically motivated. There was little he wouldn't do in his quest for power to move up.

The only thing stronger than his addiction to moving up was his dread of moving in the opposite direction. For Herod, *down* was the ultimate four-letter word. Despite his vast resources, Herod suffered the disease common to many people obsessed with power: He was plagued by insecurity and fear. He turned paranoia into an art form, mental illness into an institution. He devoted enormous energy to protecting himself from the possibility of his downfall. With an elaborate network of spies, he allowed precious little to escape his notice and never hesitated to respond to threats with violence. When he came into power as the governor of the region, several bands of troublemakers were wreaking havoc in the hillsides of Galilee. Without batting an eyelash, Herod captured the leader of the most celebrated marauder band and had him tortured and executed—slowly—in the town square. The plan "worked." The rebels were never seen again during Herod's reign.

As added defense, Herod commissioned tens of thousands of slaves to build a dozen or so emergency fortresses, all heavily armed and well provisioned, in case of a coup attempt. These "hideaways" were, in some cases, entire mountains refashioned to palatial fortresses, complete with swimming pools, aqueducts, guest quarters, dining halls and recreational facilities. He also ordered the execution of any possible candidate for his office—including two of his wives and three of his sons. The execution of one of his sons he ordered on his deathbed.

Herod lived, at the very least, a consistent life. He carried a simple philosophy—Me First—to its logical and full conclusion. For the most part, it worked pretty well. Herod ruled for more than thirty years.

Until the time of Jesus Christ.

SUDDEN IMPACT

To say that Herod and Jesus, the two kings of Matthew 2, "crossed paths" is to understate the force of the text. According to a fundamental law of physics, the force of impact depends upon speed and direction. Jesus and Herod were both moving fast, from totally opposite directions. King Herod represented the world's unvarnished perspective on power: Get it, hoard it, and use it. Jesus Christ, equal with God Himself, brought a fresh and seemingly backward approach to the management of power, and said it in simple terms: Use Power for Others. For those who missed the verbal message, He painted a picture—the all-powerful Son of God nailed to a cross. That, he said, was real power, the kind that generates the stuff of eternity.

No wonder the two kings clashed. Both possessed immense power, but how they chose to use it revealed the hearts of two radically different men. One was bent on promotion, the other bended in devotion. One was a tyrant, the other a servant. One was consumed with self interest, the other focused on God and anyone other than self. One manipulated, slandered, deceived, and coerced; the other healed, touched, taught, and loved. When it came to the management of power, there was only one thing Herod and Jesus shared in common: They both believed there was nothing that bloodshed couldn't cure.

As soon as Herod heard of Jesus' birth, he wanted Him dead. He called into power all of his resources to accomplish the task. At first, it seemed like no contest at all. Nobody messed with King Herod. Better said: Nobody messed with him and kept his head. Rarely in history was a battle between kings so dismally stacked. Herod the Intimidating, with power, resources, and armies; Jesus, nursing on His mother's breast.

The command of death went out from Herod, as cold and steely as the swords that would soon strike. When we read of the massacre in Matthew 2, it is easy to separate ourselves from the horror of the reality. But picture the soldiers riding up on horseback, breaking down the doors of the homes in Bethlehem, and running their spears through those little baby boys—right in front of their mothers and fathers. Can you imagine the sense of terror, fury, and helplessness that swept through the land?

WHO, ME?

Herod the Great was perhaps the ultimate oxymoron in history. Rich in what the world considers valuable, he was totally bankrupt as a human being. He was addicted to power, the greatest rush on earth, and believed that as long as he held it tight, he was invincible. In his own mind he was as high as a god, untouchable and eternal. Nothing bad could happen to him that a little deceit or a deadly sleight of hand couldn't fix.

Thank God, I can almost hear you say, that we are not like Herod. Surely his excuse to the human race was insanity. He could not think straight, like you and I. We use our power, what little we possess, mostly for the good. We try never to raise an angry hand to a child; we pay our taxes and slip in a little money to a charity or two; we go to church, and, occasionally, we play a game of bingo with an old person. Good people. We are not Herod or Hitler or any other maniac you choose to name.

Our greatest power turns out to be that we are deceitful enough to believe our own lies. But if we are honest and take a hard look inside, each of us will see little Herods staring back into our faces. Given the right situation, none of us is immune to working a little of Herod's magic. All too often we use our resources, talents, and charm to get what we want, hiding our motivation in subtlety or feigned ignorance. We know it by different names—office politics, turf wars, marital rights, parental perks. But it always points to the same thing: a misuse of power. Who of us hasn't resorted to a little manipulation with our spouse, a slight mistreatment of a co-worker competing for a promotion, or an innocent toot or two of our own horn? Which of us hasn't responded impatiently when someone "underneath" us on the pecking order asked a favor? Or responded to our kids with a thoughtless "Because I said so"?

Isn't there some Herod still kicking around somewhere inside all of us? Don't we all sometimes trade our value systems in on something a little more self-elevating? Doesn't "down" still cause feelings of fear and even anger now and then? All of us sometimes wear the face of Herod, perhaps carefully camouflaged with rosy cosmetics, but still sporting the same brutal leer. We share that part of him which would rather rule than serve, wield power than submit to authority, be honored rather than look for ways to honor others.

From the world's point of view, such behavior— which the Bible calls sin—makes perfect sense. We must not, our culture tells us, be too hard on ourselves. We have to take care of ourselves. If we don't, who will?

In this jungle of a world, the name of the game is survival. In order to keep from being eaten alive, we all have to flash an incisor now and then.

Don't we?

THE CRITICAL CHOICE

Let's be honest. Doesn't the world's way make more sense? Isn't Herod's example the logical one to follow? If we gather enough power, we need rely only on ourselves. Trust becomes a matter of the size of our biceps or our B2s, or whatever else we use to measure strength. We can place our faith in a seen plan, and keep control.

The way of Jesus seems, in comparison, almost ludicrous. If we yield power to others, we can no longer trust in ourselves. Trust becomes suddenly a matter of the size of our God. We must place our faith in an unseen hand, and divest ourselves of all sem- blance of control.

It seems, on the surface, like an easy choice. Herod, maniac that he was, was at least practical. Jesus seems less given to pragmatism. Can we really be expected to follow in the steps of a man who died on a cross at the age of thirty-three?

But there is more than the obvious. Wisdom, the Bible says, is justified by her results. In order to fully understand the opposite paths of Herod and Jesus, we must examine the end. Herod, with all his wealth, high position and possession, ended in ruin. In the final year of his life, his body was infected with disease; his pain was so bad that often in the middle of the night his screams could be heard in the palace. But there was more than the physical pain. He brooded over the fact that his death would be mourned by few. He wanted tears at the moment of his death, lots of tears. So he devised one final, desperate plan. He would bring together the top leaders of the land for a meeting in Jericho and, once they arrived, he would have the gates locked. Just before the moment of his death, he would order them all massacred. One way or another, the tears of the people would flow at Herod's death. But for political reasons, his plan backfired and the leaders were released. Herod died alone. He is despised in history.

Jesus, after a life of poverty and lowly position, descended yet further—to a rough-hewn wooden cross. His cries, like Herod's, also pierced the night. Yielding completely His power, He also died. But there is a critical difference between the deaths of Herod and Jesus. For all his power, Herod could not save himself from death, or its loneliness. Jesus could have, but He chose not to.

In life, Jesus willingly suffered—from the abuse of the Pharisees, the ignorance and hard-heartedness of His own disciples, the rejection of the people, the poverty of His family, the constant threats to His life, the betrayals of friends, the beatings—all for a single purpose: to demonstrate God's outrageous love. While Herod wielded the power of hate and self-protection, forming armies, building fortresses and killing at will, Jesus wielded the power of liberating love. He healed the sick and blind, comforted the brokenhearted, and freed the slaves of sin and death.

By yielding His power, Jesus proved His trust in God's plan. God said the downward path would lead to fulfillment and life, and Jesus believed Him. It was that trust which allowed Jesus to endure the cross "for the joy set before him." While Herod vainly schemed to escape the loneliness of a death he deserved, Jesus calmly accepted the agony of a death He didn't deserve. While Herod's body rotted in a granite grave, Jesus was resurrected in great power, glory, and yes, joy. For Jesus, the end was not the end. He became the most celebrated man in history.

Two kings with opposite messages. Herod: Follow your desires, avoid crosses, get. Jesus Christ: Serve others, pick up your cross each day, give. Only one of the kings, as it turned out, knew the pathway to joy.

Profile:
Lance Murdock

3

LANCE MURDOCK:
THE CHICAGO
BOARD OF TRADE AND
THE KINGDOM OF GOD

"I have to keep in mind that as hard as I work, and whatever I might achieve, whether it is planes, vacation homes, cars, recognition, the moment I die, it is gone. I could be doing so much more in working for God's kingdom."

—Lance Murdock

*L*ance Murdock knows that chaos is about to enter his world. After breakfast—four egg whites with mushrooms, two skim milks and oatmeal—he has just tipped Marie, his corner table waitress, given a smile, and feels that familiar crawling in his stomach. He calls it the pregame jitters, even after fifteen years. He knows by instinct, as a mouse in a snake cage might, that he has survived longer than most. At the age of forty-two, there are streaks of gray in his hair.

Murdock has no easy job. It's nearly 7 A.M. on the fourth floor of a building on the corner of Lasalle and Jackson in Chicago. Murdock, as is his custom, has been up since 3:30. Today, with the release of official government statistics, is likely to be a busy day at the Chicago Board of Trade. The animals, well intentioned or not, will be out, sniffing the air for the scent of money, closing in for a kill, hoofed in Reeboks.

These are his friends, these traders, these people who make their living by howling, by taking no prisoners. Almost everyone knows Lance. He is a legend of sorts in the 10-year Treasury Note Pit, a man revered, as a trader stated in the *Chicago Tribune Magazine*, "as a gentleman trader ... the epitome of what a trader should be." He smiles and says hello to almost everyone. Descending a stairway headed into the pits, he passes a photograph of the activity on the trading floor from a few years back. If you look closely, you can spot Murdock in the photo. If you look even closer, you can see incisors. "I was an animal back then," Murdock says, "an absolute animal."

There is still the thrill of it. The way the blood moves when fifty or a hundred contracts are traded, and ten seconds from eternity could mean a few thousand dollars, one way or the other. Adrenaline runs under cool reason like a river, breaking surface in conquest, submerging with energy. There is day-to-day, moment-to-moment uncertainty, even in the mind of a successful trader, of not knowing if you'll be worth a plugged nickel. Risk, fear, conquest, exaltation, chaos, self-control: the emotional soup of money, power, and control.

As he takes his one-by-one spot on the top row of the ten-year pit, he looks up. It is, more than anything, an exercise in survival. He knows of the potential bankruptcy, both in the wallet and the soul, of thinking he can do this alone. He stretches his arm up toward a spot near the ceiling, in the top southwest corner, to a bar about six feet long, a perch in his mind. It is here where he imagines God watching him. What he does, he knows, is both gift and responsibility.

The 7:20 opening bell rings, on the second, and the chaos begins.

Murdock has been calibrated for conquest. In temperament, history, skills, appearance: there is this quintessential feel about him, the ivory-white teeth, clenched or smiling. He is, without dipping into stereotypes, square-jawed, sturdy, and a wearer of monograms on his sleeves, with just a hint—sometimes in the eyes—of vulnerability. He is pleasant from the start, smooth with a smile, genuinely likable, and, on a bad day, potentially calculating with a compliment. Cool under pressure, tenaciously brilliant, he often seems unsure of himself, and prone to beat on himself for the things he has yet to accomplish. He is driven. And like most successful men, he is a paradox of control and unmet need: the very things that often drive him forward—challenge, recognition, and purpose—are also the products of the vacuum in his heart. And, beyond all of his self-confessed faults, he loves God.

From a very early age, he learned of power and control. He understood quickly that value could be earned: the calculations of the number of awards, titles, and honors. Growing up as the oldest of five children in a loving family in the suburbs of Pittsburgh, his parents gave him the tools for success—deeply embedded values of hard work, honesty, integrity, and the love of a challenge. Given the breadth of his abilities, Lance never really struggled. He was the captain of his football and baseball teams, class president, a member of the Honor Society, a nearly perpetual Optimist Boy of the Month. His mother, whose love brings him to tears even today, always challenged him to even greater accomplishments. When he had mostly A's on his report card, she would ask, "Why the B?" When he gained 180 yards in a game, she said, "Great, but you could have broken that one tackle." She wanted her son to reach his full potential. But something happened, some subtle twist in a young child's mind: "I learned to place my value entirely on my accomplishments," he says. Even God offered the potential for award. Week after week, he sat in the Presbyterian church, counting the number of sleeping people, so that he could get the Perfect Attendance pin. He worked with the pastor for a year so he could earn the Boy Scout God and Country award. But he had too much respect for power to completely trivialize God. Even later on in his life, during periods marked by sin, he still prayed. God was always his safety zone, his hedge against a complete breakdown of his own progress.

Lance had dreams. He wanted to be a professional football player. An all-American running back in high school, he was recruited by several major universities and chose Duke University. By the time he was a sophomore, he was a starting outside linebacker. After the first four weeks into his senior year, he was co-captain of a team that was undefeated and nationally ranked. And then trouble hit, maybe the first serious challenge of his life. Two running backs were injured. Since Lance was a running back in high school and it was the position he really wanted to play, he offered his services to the coach. He was rejected: "We need you too much on defense" was his coach's response. Murdock lost inspiration. The team finished 6–5, and Murdock was not selected in the professional draft.

Lacking alternatives, he decided to make a name for himself in business. After he graduated, he took a job and a wife. In his mind they were interconnected. His wife came from a wealthy family. It was an added incentive—pressure if you will—for Murdock to succeed. "My sole objective was to provide for my wife the kind of lifestyle that she had been accustomed to," he says. Never mind that she was not at all interested in being rich. It was rich incentive. He lasted just eleven months at his first job, a sales management position for Carnation in Jacksonville, Florida. "I was in too much of a hurry," he says. "I could see that it was going to take too long climbing up the corporate ladder. I couldn't wait; my hunger for recognition and money was too great." He quit and became a stockbroker in Durham, North Carolina. In an effort to succeed quickly, he spent most of his time working. His wife, feeling completely abandoned, had an affair. About the same time, Murdock took a trip to Chicago and visited the Board of Trade. "I walked onto the floor and I had no idea what was going on, but I knew that I wanted to be a part of it. It was invigorating, competitive, loud, exciting—in short, everything I wanted in a job." Murdock faced the two biggest challenges of his life: pushing away the threat to his marriage and moving forward to a job that promised the greatest intercourse with joy. He wanted to beat back all opponents.

The sad thing , he says, is that he really cared for his wife.

In the frenzy of the pits, Lance Murdock is a rock, unmoving except for a steady, paced chewing of gum, pen or finger to lips. He is still like a predator—calculating, eyes transfixed. He is waiting for the right moment, a single tick or two in time when, pricked with calculations and a needle of instinct in his stomach, he feels that profit is a prey.

It's hard to imagine the pits. Once the bell sounds, the world changes in a split second. From a reasonable sense of logic, order, and manners to frenetic yelling, jumping, manic asylum. It is a place where things are allowed that would get a person thrown into jail in almost any other part of civilized society. Today, the board showing 7:57:19, the market is moving. The drone of human voices, urgent and competing, clamber to a high ceiling, growing slower, grumbling, falling on the fire of a new round of voices, more urgent, more rapid. Occasionally the uninitiated can pick out a single voice out of the thousands, "DOWN 2 TICKS, 500 OFF. BID FOR 200, 200, 200!" Follow it, if you are lucky, to a man with bulging eyes and veins, but mostly it all drains into your brain, a single venom of jangling voices. Phones on the side, pockets in between the pits, add to the confusion; wires and orders come in from the world. Above the pits, in rows, like impartial angels in lab coats, they sit and punch computers, sending coolly phosphorescent green and yellow flickers: the numbers on the big boards, the slow monitors of chaos, the electronic calculations of life and death. The runners, trade checkers, and assistants—the grunts and apprentices— move like steady ants, flitting with tickets, stopping to say, "Sell 53 at 21, 19 at 20; buy 19 at 20, 20 for 4, 59 at 22" and moving on, blurring in the voices of others doing the same thing, to another helper, another spitter of numbers.

Murdock strikes quickly, arms and hands in sign language, voice erupting in bursts, jack hammering his vocal cords. He buys twenty contracts at 19. The market hovers at 19, for five to ten seconds, an eternity here. He minimizes his risk by selling ten of the contracts to a trader next to him at 19. Within two seconds the market rallies, and Murdock sells five contracts at 20. He makes roughly $150. The market continues to rally and, within a few seconds, he trades the remaining five contracts at 21. Another $300. Nearly $450 in his first trade, in less than a minute. A good way to begin the day. The day before, his first trade resulted in a loss of about $2,000.

Murdock is a scalper, a local. He trades for himself. Scalpers are paid no salaries and make no commissions. A scalper is like a man who goes into a grocery store with a list of what every item should cost. When he sees an underpriced item, he buys several units, hoping that the grocer will discover the price gap and mark it up. He then sells his items and pockets the profit. The market, through supply and demand, serves the same function as the grocer.

The pits can eat a person alive. Mostly, it is only the young that can hack it, and then usually not for long. It is, more than anything else, a compression, an intensification of a value system. In a word, money— compressed into a few seconds. Everything, it seems, has been designed to anticipate the pressure. The architecture is predominantly solid squares—the tiles, the high lights, the massive, symmetrical boards, the room, the squares of the cube. The jackets of the traders: red, yellow, psychedelic—the groupings of order and rank and company. But still the pressure, the chaos, seems to close in, seeping into the pores like an acid. It is an impartial world. For every winner, there is a loser. Guess right, and you survive. Guess wrong, and it may mean back to a desk job.

There is a physical edge, a kind of knotting of energy that comes with the pressure. When the market is hot, bodies press one to another, front to back, looking for a spot to yell, like some bizarre ice breaker at a singles club. Vocal cords are screamed raw. Varicose veins appear in young skin. In the energy, traders are injured, suffer fainting spells, fight one another, sometimes with their fists, even soil themselves, and still the trading continues.

Five out of six traders are gone within two years. Either burned out or broke, often the victims of themselves and certainly bowing under the pressure.

It is nearing lunch. Lance Murdock, even after fifteen years, is kicking himself. He's up about $6,000, but he feels he should be up another three or four grand. If there's one thing he has learned, you have to hit and maximize when you can. For there is always the trouble of tomorrow.

About midnight on a zero-degree night in December of 1980, Lance Murdock left his flat in downtown Chicago and took his seven-month-old puppies for a walk to the park. Rottweilers: he had always admired them; their strength reminded him of power; their devotion struck a chord of longing. As soon as he and his wife separated and he moved out, he needed companionship.

The world that he had so carefully and meticulously structured had fallen apart. A divorce was pending. He was nearly $400,000 in debt and on the verge of bankruptcy.

Up to this point, everything had happened pretty much as expected. At least those things that were under his control. He had moved to Chicago, worked as a stockbroker during afternoons and evenings, and spent time at the Board of Trade during the days. Making contacts, learning the system, studying the pros. Unlike many men obsessed with a dream, Murdock was calculating and in no hurry. He wanted to do it right. He began to save the required $120,000 to purchase a full trading pass to the floor.

In July of 1977, he took to the floor for the first time. The first few weeks were easy, almost comically so. He made $8,000 in the first month, and he couldn't have been more pleased with himself. His value was rising. Next month brought him somewhere nearer reality. He lost $16,000 and had only a few grand left to his name. But even that was nothing for Murdock. It shook him up, true, but he was built for a challenge. He geared down, sought advice, picked his spots, studied success, and learned patience and discipline. Within three years time, he was in the seven figures.

He had achieved his dreams. "I thought I was king of the hill," he says. He had time and money and respect. The name Lance Murdock began to mean something, even to himself. Still there were those nagging personal problems. In his marriage, the roles had reversed. Lance was the one who felt abandoned, he says. Because he was working the grain markets, which are open less than four hours a day, he had plenty of time on his hands. He wanted to taste the fruit of his labors—travel to exotic places, play with expensive toys, buy a bigger house. His wife wanted none of it. She was working forty to fifty hours a week and enjoying it. She had little interest in the things that her husband's money could buy. For Lance, it was a personal insult: How dare she spurn his great conquest of the marketplace by refusing to enjoy the good life that he had worked so hard, so skillfully, to provide for her?

In Lance's mind, there was still the affair. He never got over it. He had lost her, his ultimate possession, to another man. Even if it was over, there still was the bitter taste in his mouth. They began to grow in different directions. Lance was still determined to enjoy his success, even if she did not want to. He traveled to Myrtle Beach for golf, Las Vegas for gambling, Florida for the sun. By himself, with single male friends, and, then, with other women. He became a master of the chronic lie. "It became infectious," he says. "I ran our marriage right into the ground. I didn't even care."

About the only thing Murdock lacked was a sense of humility. His was a conceit under control, wearing a mask of decency and reputation, the very worst kind. "It was a planned conceit," Murdock says. "I knew my objectives." He felt invincible.

And then, against his most controlling efforts, Murdock's world began to fall apart. He was separated from his wife in late 1979. In November of 1980 as he was once again approaching seven figures, that magical number of mastery, disaster struck. As a scalper, Murdock had made his trades mostly out of instinct and in a very quick period of time. He decided to try position trading, which requires the study of a commodity, taking a position, and allowing it to run for a long period of time, usually weeks or months. It is risky business.

"I knew the top position traders at the Board of Trade and they were making hundreds of thousands over a period of weeks or months," he says. With his ego at full staff, Murdock thought he could do the same. He took a position on a soybean spread. He studied weather and pricing charts. In the first couple of weeks, he had earned $200,000 on his position. "I thought, 'This is unbelievable. Why am I working my rear end off, trading all day, fighting and yelling, buying and selling, when I do this thing, and in a couple of weeks I have a couple of hundred grand?'" He let his position run. Into the ground. In the next eight days, the position turned against him. He lost his $200,000 profit, about $750,000 in his trading account, and was about $400,000 in debt. In all, the position had cost him about $1.3 million. In just over one week.

That is how he found himself in a Chicago park, broken, with his Rottweiler puppies, the dogs of power. He remembers the wind ripping inside of him, somewhere near his soul, leaving him shaking, empty, and cold. "I had run everything into the ground," he says. "I was going through a divorce, I had a negative net worth. I didn't know if I was coming or going. I had no social value, I just kept thinking that I wasn't worth a nickel." Economically, socially, and morally he was headed toward bankruptcy.

In the empty, open field, the winter ran through him. Everything was in ruin, the dark blue of shame. The dogs nudged forward, hoping to break through his pain. Murdock cried.

_____

When the Exchange slows, it crawls. As the clock reads 1:12:36, the boredom prowls, settling on bleeding nerves like cool blue water in a fresh wound. Lance stands firm in the ten-year pit, chewing a stick of gum, breaking into the bubble of a conversation around him. Instead of the grind of frenzied voices, there is a buzz, like the winding of a clock, just an inch or two from tension. The traders must survive this, too. One sits crouched on the steps up to a pit, reading an editorial in *USA Today*, "Should Gambling Be Legalized?" Another whistles a song, sounds like "Unforgettable" or "Here Comes the Sun." The bathrooms and the phones are in full use. The scraps of conversation are as many as the torn pieces of paper on the trading floor. "I'm convinced," says one trader behind a phone, "that every deviant thing your mind could think of, someone, somewhere is already doing it." Another complains of season tickets for the Cubs' games, deep along third base, putting her almost in left field. Two guys along the rail share father stories: "My son just had his second birthday party; he got chocolate icing in his ears." Another rubs his head, "Got in late last night, gotta stop doing that. I never find what I'm looking for anyway."

The energy is the thing that comes through. Even when time is broken down, crawling along in thick-liquid seconds, and the mad rush of voices slows, the softer, slightly exposed tones of pain and longing spring. In the pits, there is a fierce movement of life. The money, if one could hear in between the bottom lines, is not the real issue.

Slowly Lance Murdock came to the realization that the real disaster in his life was not losing nearly $1.4 million, it was the bankruptcy of his thinking. It was the belief that he could build for himself an indestructible world, an environment where nothing could get through—failure, fear, the thief in the middle of the night. If he could stack circumstances—his bank account, his trading reputation, his successes—then he could always count his own self-worth. The plan backfired. Looking back through disaster, he could see that all of his successes did not add up to much past zero. It was not that he was a bad person: He had always been likable and genuinely caring. It was that his hopes had been in the wrong places. "I realized that I placed my value and importance as a human being on superficial successes. I saw that I was really no better as a person."

Even then, when God was still on his string, Murdock began to make changes. He realized that what he did as a trader was a gift. He had responsibility to develop that gift and, somehow, place a different value on it. He could no longer judge his worth by the number of cars, homes, and private planes he owned. He had learned a fragile grace.

He also learned about giving. Three of his friends pooled their funds to help him out of debt. They did not charge interest, and they expressed confidence in him. They asked that he retire from position trading and return to day trading. His friends believed in him to the tune of $400,000. It touched Murdock. In some way, it was as if God Himself had broken through. It was hard to understand and impossible to forget.

Gradually Murdock recovered. Within three years or so, he was back into the seven figures, a director of the Chicago Board of Trade, and slightly less confused about life. He still prayed and now read the Bible a half hour a day, still the self interested believer, but with greater or at least more restless questions: Who is God? What does He want out of me? In 1984 his parents came to visit. Solid Christians, they looked for a church to attend on Sunday.

They happened upon a church that looked like a corporate office building, Willow Creek Community Church. They loved it. Murdock's mom, always the challenger, asked Lance to go with them. He reluctantly agreed. He was planning to relive his youth, counting the number of people who had fallen asleep; instead, he was overwhelmed with a presence of God. The faith that he saw there was vital, strong, powerful. His mom sensed that her son would be changed. And she cried.

Murdock continued to attend, interested and at the same time skeptical. He sat in the first row of the back balcony, nearest the exit. He was analyzing, waiting patiently for the catch. Gradually he started to tithe. Eventually he got a call from the senior pastor, asking him out for lunch. Murdock thought he would soon find the catch: the church was interested in him for his money. During the lunch, he waited for the pastor to thank him for his generous giving. It never came. Instead came the questions about his spiritual and moral life. The pastor learned that he was living with his girlfriend. He challenged him, in no uncertain terms, to live a life honoring to Christ. "He lowered the boom on me," Murdock says. "If words would have been a knife, I would have been in little pieces." But instead of being offended, Murdock felt cared for. He had finally found people who didn't give two bits for his money or reputation, but only cared about his growth in Jesus Christ.

Since that time, there have been significant changes in Murdock's life. After separating from his girlfriend, Lynda, and living celibate lives, they are now married. They have four children (two from Lynda's previous marriage and two of their own). It is obvious when you enter their home that Murdock's priorities have changed. On the baby grand piano are pictures of his family and children. As he looks out over the pond in their front yard, he talks of the two oldest boys and fishing. He shows off the white fresh room of McKelle, their two-year-old daughter, with a splash of pride. Campbell, the newborn, can make him giggle like a schoolboy.

"I am so grateful," says Murdock. "God has changed my life around. I can't begin to tell you how blessed I feel. Through Lynda and the kids, God is teaching me what it is like to be loved. God has blessed me beyond what I could have imagined. The love we share is very deep."

He has changed his focus as a trader. No longer does he wish to be the "all-conquering hero of the Board of Trade." He seeks to be responsible. He has for the first time in his life a sense of "deep contentment" that comes from his relationship with God. He has developed a structure of accountability—his "personal board of directors"—so that he will continue to maintain integrity in his personal and spiritual life. He is loosening the hold that possessions once had on his life.

But that is not to say that all is well with Murdock. In some ways, his relationship with God has brought chaos into his life. There are, deep within him, two value systems at battle. One says conquer. The other says yield. One says get. The other says give. One says external matters are what are important: dollar bills, achievements, titles, recognition. The other says the internal realities are critical: faith, love, and hope. Murdock is willing to change, but the work is difficult. Because of the conflicting mindsets—the old perspective versus the new perspective—Murdock's life is often complex.

He freely admits that he is still driven to do and to earn. Old habits die hard. In addition to his job as a day trader, he is a co-owner and partner of a health insurance company in the northwest suburbs of Chicago. The business takes a good deal of his time. His life is scheduled from 3:30 A.M. until at least 5 P.M. Family and church are sometimes sacrificed.

On almost every level, Murdock struggles for a balance. Can he be a success at the Board of Trade without compromising faith and character? "A lot of times," he says, "as the intensity levels go up, your ethics want to go down. It's a constant battle." He feels an intense responsibility to represent Christ. Many of the traders have noticed the difference in his demeanor. He is no longer an animal. They ask and he tells them about the new priorities in his life. He knows that he has a rare opportunity to bring the gospel to people mostly absorbed in self-promotion.

Each day Murdock faces the difference between the two kingdoms—of man and of God. He is faced with this question: What is success? Real success? "I have to keep in mind that as hard as I work, and whatever I might achieve, whether it is planes, vacation homes, cars, or recognition—the moment I die, it is gone. I could be doing so much more in working for God's kingdom. What you do for God's kingdom is eternal. Eternity is unfathomable."

There is a stripping process. Murdock is learning to ask questions: Can I maintain possessions and still be effective as a Christian? What is the line between need, blessing, and excess? Could I still serve Christ if I had nothing? Is a jet okay, or a mansion, or a vacation home? Murdock tithes faithfully, contributes to a few foundations, and gives to the benevolence board at the church. He wants to do more. He believes there are "excesses" in his life that could be yielded in an effort to better advance the kingdom.

He says he is moving slowly. By doing good, he does not want to shift into reverse. Back into the "do and earn" mentality. "There is a gray line," he says, "between living our faith out of gratitude versus trying to earn points with God because of the things you have done for Him." He doesn't want to go back to earning perfect attendance awards.

In spite of all the growth in his life he still feels disconnected. "I feel that I have been blessed with so many capabilities and resources, and yet I don't feel that I'm living up to what I can do for God's kingdom. To one who is given much, much will be required. I feel a yearning or gnawing inside of me."

Such, he says, is the starting point for the path that leads down. Into chaos and God's control.

It is one minute until the closing bell. There is the pandemonium, the flurry of screams and last-second trades. Murdock has sold contracts and broken even on a last-minute deal. A few seconds later, the market rallies. He could have made a considerable profit. A few years back, he would have been upset. Now there is just the hint of a smile on his face.

Above him, at a spot near the ceiling, in the top southwest corner, there is a bar about six feet long, unnoticed by most. It is there that Murdock imagines God watching him. It is, Murdock says, a matter of perspective.

COMMITMENT

4

LIFE OUT OF
THE COMFORT ZONE

"[He] made himself nothing."

—*Philippians 2:7*

*J*esus Christ made himself nothing. There is something troubling about the idea. Maybe it's the word
"nothing." There is an uneasy combination of emptiness and violence about the word, a dreadful stripping
of what is. There is nothing good about nothing. We
can't take nothing to the bank, to the beach, or to the
self-esteem seminar. With nothing, we would be
laughed out of places like boardrooms and awards
banquets. If we want to prove our value, if we want to
be *some*body, we have to acquire or accomplish *some*-
thing. *Nothing* is for *no*bodies.

But it's more than that. Look again: Jesus Christ
made Himself nothing. That implies willful action.

Jesus deliberately stripped Himself of everything—His divine rights and privileges—and crossed the unthinkable chasm between God and man.

Try to imagine the span of that chasm. Try to measure the descent from heaven to earth with a tape measure or an odometer or with the speed of light. Miles and millennia will fade into eternity. Find another Einstein, run a new equation, and let the computer buzz and whir. Minds and chips will melt. The distance that Jesus Christ descended is simply incalculable.

But distance is not the only descent to be measured. There is also the descent of essence, of being: The unlimited God became limited man. Before the descent, Jesus stood at the center of the cosmos: the focal point of all praise, the Creator of all things and beings, the energy and power that holds everything together. Jesus Christ was not an assistant, not an eternal second-in-command or heir to a never-to-be-vacated throne. Philippians 2:6 tells us that He was "in very nature God." It was Jesus Christ, equally with the Father and the Holy Spirit, who created the world and reigns from eternity past, and to whom the angels bowed and cried "Holy, holy, holy" in Isaiah's spectacular vision of worship in Isaiah 6. Jesus Christ is God.

But He chose to descend, to relinquish His divine rights. Suddenly He had to use doors, ride mules, eat and sleep. His muscles got sore. He said, "Okay, Dad, yes, Mom, whatever you say." He traded worship for curses and praise for spit in His face. "Holy, holy, holy," for "Hey, Jew boy." Imagine the omniscient, omnipresent, omnipotent second Person of the Trinity yielding to the binding restrictions of the flesh.

Heaven to earth, God to man ... but that still does not measure the full descent of Jesus Christ. He had yet to face the cross: rough, splintered, stark against the sky, and bloodstained. When Christ died, it was His only possession; He owned it through the nails. Abandoned, broken, forsaken of men and of God, He was pulled from the cross and buried. There were no wills to contest; Jesus had no homes or land or money. There were no kingdoms to pass on; He had only a handful of followers, and even they had scattered. He had no children and left no written legacy. From the world's viewpoint, Jesus had descended as low as a man—to say nothing of God—could go.

But there was one more downward step, in heaven's eyes the deepest descent of all: from sinless to sin stained. Into Jesus' soul flooded the hate of every lie, the evil of every impure thought, the venom of every cruel word, the tragedy of every good deed left undone. And the Father, in His holiness, burned against His Son. Jesus plunged into the fiery ocean of God's undiluted wrath against sin. Truly, He could go no lower.

When one comes to understand the violence of the descent, one is even more amazed by the verse: Jesus *made* Himself nothing. He was not pushed, threatened, or coerced; nor was His descent an accidental fall. It was the result of an unwavering, willful commitment to divine logic. Step by deliberate step, Jesus *chose* to move from the pinnacle of creation to the debasement of the cross. From the time He left heaven, He followed only one direction, and that in the straightest of paths: down. He knowingly and actively embraced a life of giving, serving, losing, and dying.

TOUGH CHOICES FOR US

What was, and is, really hard for Jesus' followers to swallow is that we are called to do the same. To make ourselves nothing. By dying to selfish interests, we are to follow Jesus down the ladder, step by step. But downward mobility is not something that just happens to us. Like Jesus, we must make active, willful, day-to-day decisions to move down. And like Jesus, we must use God's logic. We must believe that as painful as it sometimes feels, descending is the only way to greatness.

From the world's perspective, the road that Jesus followed—the same road we are told to walk— made no sense; it was *non*sense. What kind of God would demand such foolish acts of self-destruction? And why would any sane person follow such walking orders? There is a single answer to both questions. Love. The story of the God who voluntarily demoted Himself, who down-scaled and lost on purpose, who died so that the penalty of your sin and mine would be paid for all eternity is, above all else, a love story. God asked His Son to descend for the sake of love. Jesus obeyed for the sake of love.

And we, His followers and the recipients of His love, are called to do the same. When asked about the two greatest commands, Jesus replied: to love God and to love others. That is what motivated Jesus, and that is what is to motivate us.

But again, as with Jesus, the descent love requires does not just happen. Each of us must make active—and often costly—choices.

One couple in our church, feeling trapped by the demands of their large "dream" home, decided to sell it and move into a smaller house that required less attention. The goal was to have more time and resources to build relationships. "Christ was on the throne of our lives," said Sue, "but materialism was (sitting) right next to Him, eating up our lives." The move to downscale is often difficult for others to accept. Sue's two teenage daughters, for example, find it difficult to explain to their friends in the affluent northwest suburbs of Chicago why their parents would make such a decision. And being misunderstood and even criticized is hard to take. But the family has no intention of returning to the bondage of their previous lifestyle.

Another young woman, Jodi, decided to take a downward step after taking a vacation. On a trip to a tourist paradise, her bus passed through miles of poverty-stricken Mexico. It was the first time Jodi had come face-to-face with such impoverishment. "There I was," she says, "on my way to a posh hotel, zooming past hundreds of destitute people." When she returned home, she made a conscious decision to do something. Now, once a week, she volunteers her skills as a physical therapist to serve the inner city poor in Chicago. "I had never driven into the city before," says Jodi, recalling her fears. "It was frightening and it still is . . . (but) I refuse to let fear stop me from going."

Frank, with a wife and six children, also found himself facing a painful decision. The company he worked for—one of the nation's top video game manufacturers—was producing products Frank increasingly felt uneasy with. Many of the video games he sold displayed and promoted sex, violence, and bigotry. Finally one game went "over the limit." It was a difficult decision for him to quit. He had an impressive salary, a prestigious title, a generous expense account, and a good deal of security . . . not to mention a family of eight to feed. How could he give all that up? How would he be able to feed his family? Frank finally quit, following the painful road down.

Time and again, I run into people who have felt a leading to descend, to downscale, to accept a demotion, for the sake of advancing the kingdom of Christ. While I have never met a person who was sorry he or she descended, nearly everyone I meet who has followed such a leading has faced a certain degree of discomfort, because many of the choices were downright painful. It isn't easy to trade Adam's prayer, "Not Your will, but mine," for Jesus' prayer, "Not my will, but Yours." Moving down involves humility, brokenness, dependency, servanthood, and obedience—none of which come to any of us naturally. We are all more comfortable with the status quo.

THIS *IS LIFE TO THE FULL?*

Not long ago a woman stopped me in the hallway at church and thanked me profusely for forcing her to move out of the comfort zone. "I spent most of my life trying to arrange circumstances, carefully and conservatively, so I could live comfortably, safely, with few surprises and minimal inconveniences. Now I'm learning that loving isn't always comfortable. Sometimes it leads me down unexpected turns and gets terribly inconvenient. But it's a much more exciting, fulfilling way to live. I never again want to get stuck in the comfort zone!"

Yet isn't that where most people—even many sincere Christians—live their day-to-day lives? Don't we tend to focus on Bible passages that guarantee safety, security, peace, victory, and reward? Aren't those the ones we memorize and put on wall plaques? We tend to overlook or "soften" those passages that would jeopardize or threaten our comfort. The verses that pierce and cut and expose and challenge us to downward mobility seldom make the calligraphy plaques.

Author Scott Peck observes that people will go to unbelievable lengths to avoid experiencing pain and discomfort—in marriage, parenting, the marketplace, and almost every area of life. Instead of dealing with problems squarely, which might cause conflict, people often ignore them or divert their energies elsewhere—sports, alcohol, sex, shopping, eating—and create a fairly convincing image of peace and comfort. But the peace is false and the comfort is costly. It is bought at the expense of reality and personal growth.

Only over time do we realize that this comfort zone of our careful making is not what we really wanted after all. Comfort, the absence of pain, does not lead to fulfillment; in fact, it often works against it. There is an irony here. Positive change, spiritual growth, character advances, relational progress require pain, conflict, or tension as a kind of fuel for change. Athletes say, "No pain, no gain." Businessmen echo, "No guts, no glory." Spiritually speaking, the same principles apply. We need to realize that the kind of life "to the full" that Jesus promised His followers in John 10:10 is not found along the upward path toward the comfort zone, but along the downward path toward challenge, tough choices, painful growth, and obedience.

In John 20 Jesus appeared to His disciples and showed them the scars in His hands and sides. Then He issued this command: "Peace be with you! As the Father has sent me, I am sending you." Doesn't that seem like a strange juxtaposition? "I am sending you to a life of scars and death. But don't worry, peace will go with you."

The point is this: Fullness of life does not involve avoidance of pain but rather the courage to *move through* pain. The road down is a path that cuts through flesh and bone. Downward mobility is not just a matter of how much money we give away, but how much of ourselves we yield, how much of the sin and excess in our lives we are willing to tear away. It is an attitude marked by strength of character. And we do not grow in character without pain.

When Jesus walked the earth, He had an eye for character flaws and was committed to correcting them. He was constantly setting up mirrors that reflected people's greed, pride, dishonesty and immorality; His words often caused discomfort and guilt. He wasn't an easy person to have around—and He still isn't. Through the Bible Jesus reveals us for who we are. He's still asking us to change, still demanding painful acknowledgment and difficult work.

THE LAND OF BLAND?
OR THE GREAT ADVENTURE?

When we are challenged by others or by the Spirit about our honesty or kindness or morality or selfishness, what do we do? Do we crawl back into our comfort zones of self-deception and denial, or do we face our need to grow and change? Those moments of decision, when we feel the sweat behind our collars—the heat of the Spirit—are critical moments. They demand a conscious movement of the will. There are two choices: back into the comfort zone or forward with the leading of the Spirit. One seems safe. The other involves risk. One asks little except sufficiency. The other asks everything in trust. One is comfortable and fortified. The other is exposed and unknown.

Will you hide in the comfort zone or follow the leading of the Spirit? Before you answer, there's something you should know. There's a trick answer, or at least an unexpected one. The comfort zone, as it turns out, is not all that comfortable. In fact, it is not anything it is cracked up to be. And the leading of the Holy Spirit, in turn, is not all that painful. The truth is, if we let the fear of pain or failure keep us in our comfort zone, we will continually dwell in the land of the familiar—the whining humdrum of predictable days and months and years. But if we are willing to move through our fear, God has promised us that we will live in the realm of the supernatural—the daily and unpredictable adventure of a Spirit-led life, filled with miraculous leadings and experiences we could never have imagined.

It takes a willful, conscious decision to move out of the comfort zone and down the paths of greatness. Each day the Spirit calls us to follow, to descend: to call and encourage a friend, share Christ with a neighbor, serve, spend time with our families, give money to someone in need, reconcile a relationship, ask forgiveness, admonish a friend—to make ourselves nothing so we can love better. And that is where the pain can come in. When the Spirit asks us to put aside selfish desires, inconvenience ourselves, and crawl out of our comfort zones, the requests always hide a thorn.

The only way we learn the art of moving forward in the face of pain is by doing. The logic of moving out of our comfort zones only ceases to be illogical when we act. Once we make the move, once we start taking those downward steps, we find the joy of abandoning ourselves to God's will and protection. We find there *is* fulfillment in loving others. The comfortable life we plan is downright dull—truly the Land of Bland—compared to the Great Adventure God has in store for us.

Profile:
Dr Jim Judge

5

DR. JIM JUDGE:
INTO AFRICA

Jim is coming to the growing realization that security—real security that doesn't depend on a correct arrangement of circumstances—comes only by not trying to secure it. Rather, it comes by giving—of control, of plans, and, above all, of yourself.

*I*t started at twilight, the black clouds dancing with speed and rain. Now, with a wake of fog settling into the Rift Valley of Kenya near Mount Longonot, which just happens to be an active volcano, they pinprick the sky, swarming, gathering, beating a dead rhythm with their wings, gaining speed in flight. And finally, as if in search of Pharaoh himself, they descend on Jim Judge's backyard.

There's something you should understand. Dr. Jim Judge, as a whole, likes to play it safe, low key, as in Mr. Rogers's sweaters and three-year plans. Watching flying termites like the kind now plink, plink, plinking against his window is not how he would

script a perfect evening. You would think that this—
this scene from Revelation or Stephen King—would be
enough to put Jim Judge over the edge.

Maybe not. He is up during dessert—brownies
tonight—and in between conversations with his oldest
daughter, Emily, he bats the little termites with a fly
swatter. "Doo-Doo heaven," he says, repeating over
and over the Swahili word for insects, "Doo-Doo." One
of the Doo-Doos drops onto a plate. "Oh gross, Dad!"

This is funny. Dr. Jim Judge has come a long way
to be here, this moment of a belly laugh: certainly, the
distance between the western suburbs of Chicago and
the Kijabe Medical Center in Africa, not only in terms
of miles, but across those invisible and immeasurable
separations of language, culture, and history. That
much is obvious. The greater distance has been crossed
in his personal journey of faith.

"I am a planner," Judge says. "I like to give God
blueprints to work with." But it was not Judge's plan to
be in Africa, at least not now. He alone was certainly
not the architect of a series of circumstances that led
him and his family to sell their dream home in an affluent suburb and eat the cost of a year's worth of missionary work in a country halfway around the world.
That kind of risk taking is not at all like Jim Judge. His
commitment, more times than not, had been to play it
safe.

But leave it to God.

Judge, at the very least, has had the good sense
to go along for the ride. Along the way, he has learned
a lot about obedience, commitment, and stripping himself of his "needs" for security, safety, and comfort. "It's
not just a one-time decision we make," he says. "It's the

hundreds of decisions we make every day." More and more, he has learned to trust in God.

It is the kind of obedience that leads to freedom. One that can laugh in the middle of all the Doo-Doo.

There is something about Jim Judge, maybe the way his synapses fire, and the resulting eruptions of unexpected and slightly disarming words. "A dynamic, little pipsqueak of a woman," he is likely to say. Maybe it's the way he can whine his vowels, slowly through the nose, as if he hated to give them up, Oooh, Eeeyh: the forewarning of a punch line, the often off-center backwash of his own humor. Maybe it's his appearance: a receding hairline, a slight overbite, a certain look in the eyes—the unsettling mixture of adult and child and the sparks between automatic brilliance and a need to charm.

His dad was a spectraphotographer; he made instruments that analyzed the spectrum of light. To understate: He was brilliant. Jim, too, was bright—he had skipped two grades by the time he graduated from high school. But he felt he was never quite *that* bright. His dad, a conservative with a solid commitment to the work ethic and integrity, seemed to know something about everything. To complicate matters, his family moved a great deal. By the time he was in the tenth grade, he had been to ten different schools.

Jim says he has always wrestled with insecurity. He chose to be a doctor for two basic reasons. First, he had finally found something that his father didn't know anything about. And second, he would never have to worry about paying the bills. Although he was a deeply sensitive person, altruism didn't drive his decision to be a physician; neither did money or status. It was more a need to feel unshakable, or at least accepted.

Growing up in the tail end of the sixties, he watched the cultural revolution from the sidelines. "I fell into the category of those who watched other people take it on the head."

Most of his plans revolved around this idea: Don't do anything careless. His security depended upon keeping the apple cart from wobbling: not too fast, no sharp corners, and never leave the wide and paved road. Stick to the map. But as hard as he tried, no matter the precautions, the wheels kept threatening to fall off. There was always this annoying discrepancy in his life: his external appearance never matched his internal reality. On the outside, he was the good-natured, highly popular fraternity brother, the kind that dated sorority queens. On the inside was gross, intense insecurity. "I would lie in bed at night and just worry about all the possible things that could go wrong." He would, he says, never fall asleep until his digital clock read 1:11. An existential quirk, uniquely his.

And then, all of a sudden, there was God to deal with. His sorority queen girlfriend had gone and found Jesus, of all people. Jim, at first, blamed it on the funny cigarettes she smoked. When she told him that she had a personal relationship with Jesus Christ, Jim's response was: "That's like saying you have a personal relationship with a Hershey Bar." That kind of talk made no sense. Jesus Christ died 2,000 years ago. There's not much security, he reasoned, in praying to a dead man.

But he was curious. There were changes, real and deep, in his girlfriend. In order to "end the nonsense," he asked her for a Bible so that "he could point out all the inconsistencies." As hard as he studied, he could find none; in fact, it was often he who felt inconsistent: "The words were leaping off the page at me." He went to church and was pierced. Finally, one evening he could not study or sleep, so he prayed. "Lord, if You are the author of change, then I want You in my life because I need change in my life."

Over the next couple of months, he says he experienced "small but very real change." For one thing, his spirit began to settle. Rarely did he see the digits of his clock move to 1:11.

———————

Just outside of the Kijabe Medical Center in Kenya, in a cemetery, the early morning light is cool, a Jupiter orange falling on the tombs. Walking on a dirt path, Dr. Jim Judge is on his way to work. The names of the early missionaries, their short lives etched in stone, whisper of history, of sacrifices that cannot be shaken.

Crispus is the keeper of the cemetery. "Hello," Jim says. Blind in one eye and near-blind in the other, Crispus is forced to tilt his head carefully, slightly back and to the right in order to see. He is very poor. "Hello," he returns, the color in his words slowing in the dampness of the morning. As Jim heads toward the hospital, Crispus is left to his tasks of shovel and axe, the plots of future resurrection.

As he enters the hospital, Dr. Judge begins his rounds. In the course of the next few hours, he will see patients in the pediatric ward, the maternity ward, the premature baby nursery, the adult wards (private and not-so-private), the outpatient clinic, and the surgical unit. Jim is one of four doctors currently at the hospital, which can serve up to 220 patients. An average of 300 are seen each day as outpatients. "You become a specialist at everything here," Jim says. He is oncologist, pediatrician, obstetrician, radiologist, surgeon—you name it. Outside of hospitals in Nairobi, which are prohibitively expensive and more than an hour away assuming you have a car, the Kijabe Medical Center offers the only reliable medical care in the area.

The hallways, bathed in pastel light of aqua green and delicate raspberry, are littered with the wings of termites, white and frail. They cover the floor, looking like the veiny kind of whirligigs that some trees throw for seed. Today it's more of the same—disease and some healing and more disease.

For example, in the N ward of the pediatrics unit—a sparse room of eight steel-framed beds and generic sheets with black stenciled letters, KMC PAED— Jim makes his clinical observations. An eight-year-old girl who has been vomiting worms; a three-year-old with severe pneumonia; a retarded child in his early teens with a bacterial infection in the lining of his heart; a ten-year-old boy who weighs thirty pounds; a baby with malaria; a two-year-old girl, looking all of six months, probably with AIDS. With cool distraction, Dr. Judge fires off instructions: a list of medicines, tests, and procedures. An IV for him, an X-ray for her, a blood count, an upper GI.

When he can, he tries to see with a clinical eye. Otherwise, he sees this: a beautiful young woman gently kissing her two-year-old baby girl, both matched in a light blue, both with AIDS; a boy, unable to keep down food, starving to death alone; a mother holding onto her retarded teenage son during still another seizure; a baby girl, with big brown eyes, vomiting on the hand-knit sweater with too-long sleeves; a baby girl, fighting for breath, dying from pneumonia, who, given the proper technology, might have lived to have grandchildren. And that's just in one unit of one floor of one ward. Emotionally, Jim says, "You have to try and protect yourself."

Especially in this country. As Jim examines people in the outpatient unit, he explains the medical conditions of Kenya. In the immediate view of the medical center, the mortality rate in the first year of life is one in four. The two biggest causes of those deaths are pneumonia and dehydration. Much of the disease is the result of bad drinking water and poor diet and, given proper resources and education, preventable. But that's not the *really* bad news. AIDS is. Out of those patients tested at the medical center, one of four—more than 25 percent—were positive for the HIV virus. For "healthy" people wishing to donate blood to the hospital, one in ten tested positive. A realistic estimate, Jim believes, is that one in every eight Kenyans carries the HIV virus. During the next five years, it is estimated that more than 70 million people in east and central Africa will die of complications from AIDS. "This is the next thing to genocide," Jim says. The explosion of AIDS, in turn, has increased the occurrence of other diseases: tuberculosis, typhoid, cholera, and pneumonia.

All afternoon long at the outpatient clinic, the patients flow into Dr. Jim Judge's office. A four-year-old with measles and pneumonia. A woman with pain in her breast, probably cancer, not much that can be done. A little boy with a history of severe eczema, a skin disease, has a thick crust of fungus on his skin. In the onslaught of disease, Dr. Judge tries to remember names.

Like Naumi. "Hey, Naumi, how are you, little girl? You're not feeling so well today, are you?" Naumi is two. She has a fever of 101 degrees and has a chest infection, probably pneumonia. Jim faces a judgment call, one of hundreds he will make today. Should Naumi be hospitalized? He decides yes, orders penicillin, chest X-rays, a blood sugar count. Gently translated through a nurse, he explains the situation to Naumi's mother, who cradles her sick child in her arms.

After his conversion to Christianity, Jim Judge's plans changed: He began to include God in them. But in some ways, he felt even more pressure to come up with the *right* plan. He now had the added responsibility to make sure that he was in God's will. Control was essential.

It is no surprise that after beginning a relationship with Jesus Christ, Jim considered scrapping plans to go to medical school to enroll in seminary. He was so serious about the idea that, around a Thanksgiving table, he told his dad of his seminary plan, who, upon hearing the news, went upstairs. Eventually, through a unique leading of God, Jim gave up that plan and came up with a new one: the missions plan. It happened innocently enough. First came the excitement of ministry. Jim became involved in Campus Crusade for Christ at West Virginia University. The ministry was experiencing a major movement of the Holy Spirit; Jim was involved in the intense relationships that develop through evangelism and discipleship.

One of those relationships was with a woman named Cindy. Soon they were dating. In a couple of years, they were married. "What drew us together," says Jim, "was our love for ministry." They didn't know each other well. Jim, for instance, had little idea how much God would use Cindy to shake his life.

First there was her love for missions. Cindy, a Christian radical of sorts, is somewhat of a risk taker who had been actively involved in ministry for down-and-outers. For Jim, a middle-to-upper-class suburban boy, that was an unexpected and dangerous combination. Risk and compassion were two things that could cost him a good deal of his security.

Still he didn't want to be out of God's will. In medical school, he looked at missions as a logical plan for a Christian physician. "I looked at it very intellectually," Jim says. "There was a greater need overseas and greater resources in the United States." During his fourth year in medical school, and the second year of their marriage, Jim and Cindy left for their first stint overseas—Nigeria.

It did not always go smoothly. Like right from the start. When their Boeing 747 pulled up the runway in Nigeria at three in the morning in 105-degree heat, Jim looked out his window and saw a horde of sheiks in flowing white robes. As they waited outside the plane, Jim couldn't help but notice their swords. "I

thought we were going to be sacrificed immediately."
As it turned out, it was a welcoming committee for a
dignitary.

Then Jim got malaria. "Imagine the worst flu
that you have ever had in your life, plus a brain tumor." Despite the bad experiences, Jim and Cindy experienced meaningful ministry and left the door open
to returning. They waited for God's leading.

The dirt path cuts through the shambas, the
farms on the rolling hills outside of Kijabe. The
Judges—Jim and Cindy and their three children, Emily,
Katie, and Jennifer—are out for a walk. Not exactly
your typical Sunday afternoon stroll. This is the rainy
season: a fecundity of the senses, saturated greens,
blitzes of peach smells, bells and bleating, clouds that
seem to tumble and break and regather without the
movement of time. From somewhere in the hills comes
the sound of gospel, stirring, moving, drumming in cut
time, the notes of the heart falling in echoes down into
the valley.

There are no cars or televisions here, only people and animals. A young woman in a brilliant red
dress and bandanna, her face lined with streams of
sweat, carries a load of broken lumber on her back, a
support rope across her forehead. Emily and Jennifer
giggle and Katie, always the sensitive one, looks concerned. There is a boy in a Tom and Jerry sweater, another under a faded ivory-pink umbrella, the sun
breaking slowly on his face in shades of rose. There are
girls in bright and flowing dresses, reds and yellows

and greens in silk. There is, always, the crisp laughter, the bark of dogs. Life runs here on a slower clock.

The Judges have come to see Jane, one of the workers at the Kijabe missionary compound, and her five children. Cindy knows the way well. She helped Jane mud the walls of her house, which sits on a hill, surrounded by maize and the sky. By Western standards, the house is not much, a collection of mud, scrap lumber, tin, pictures from old calendars, pages from coloring books, and old church bulletins. But it is home, a good one at that, straight and true, with a rain gutter over the door.

Jane is obviously proud. In some ways, the house could be said to be symbolic of change in her life, which was at one point tragic and self-destructive. She had five children out of wedlock and secrets she did not wish to share. Jesus Christ turned her life around.

The two families sit in her "living room," an open fire heating water for chai, a chalky, sweet tea. After the mugs are handed out, Jane prays. Jennifer, one eye peeking from between fingers, looks up and smiles. Thousands of miles from her home, on the other side of the world, the extended family of Jesus Christ.

In 1981 Dr. Jim Judge entered into practice with twelve other physicians. He quickly developed a new plan. He would spend three years in private practice and then return overseas as a missionary doctor. Even though he loved his job, he didn't always see it as *real* ministry. In 1983 the Judges had the opportunity to return to Africa—this time to fill a short-term need for doctors at a medical center in Kenya. With their four-year-old and two-year-old daughters and Cindy six months pregnant, they went to Kijabe for the first time and stayed about three months. They loved the ministry.

When he returned home, Jim expected to hear from God at any moment about the direction of his life. A divine plan. But there was dead silence. In looking back, Jim is not sure what he wanted. A note on the refrigerator? A vision in the night? What he got was angry. During the next year, Jim's relationship with God began to erode in the acid of disappointment.

For a few years, the Judges were involved in important ministries. Jim taught at his church, soon became one of its leaders. But over time both Jim and Cindy found their Christianity—once vital and filled with passion—dissolving into a lifestyle. The church they were attending, although strong in teaching and biblical wisdom, often seemed inwardly focused. The spiritual fire of evangelism, the very thing that had connected the two of them in the first place, was missing.

The Judges, disconnected, began a slow, almost unnoticeable slide into materialism and busyness, the twin plagues of suburbia. There was almost this kind of subconscious reasoning: If God was going to ask them to have a ministry in the suburbs, then they would need to fit in. Or: A bigger house is an investment; we *need* to buy one if we are to be good stewards. They even resorted to reasoning framed by their tax bracket.

The Judges bought a big old house, certainly not elaborate by their community's standards, but quite comfortable. Or so they thought. Soon Cindy found herself struggling with exhaustion—the house seemed to be sucking her energy. And for Jim there was the pool. Or better, The Pool. Or, maybe even more accurately, THE POOL. Like some kind of Edgar Allan Poe nightmare, THE POOL began to make demands: feed me chlorine; get that leaf out of here; change my chemistry. There were, in fact, entire months when the family did not feel free to travel because of THE POOL. This was getting ridiculous. "When I reached seventy would I best be remembered for how clean I kept my pool?"

The phone rings, and Jim Judge has an emergency. Naumi, the little two-year-old girl he admitted into the hospital with pneumonia, is not doing well. He'd better go and have a look. When Jim arrives, Naumi is still, except for labored breathing. It is as if she is saving every ounce of energy for her next breath. Her temperature is 103.6 degrees. Naumi, Jim says, is in serious trouble. After he finds the X-ray, evaluates the blood tests, he orders an IV, oxygen, and a higher dose of penicillin. He fears that Naumi may also have malaria, although there is no real way to tell with the lack of diagnostic services. He decides to also begin treatment for malaria.

This is when it gets to Jim. Back in the States this child would not die. Here there are no guarantees. "It's like you blast kids with everything you've got." There is nothing subtle about disease in Africa. "Every disease you see in Africa is the worst case you've ever seen," Jim says. "The children are always on the worst end."

Sitting on bed Q4 of the pediatric ward, Jim explains Naumi's condition to her mother and father. "Pneumonia is very severe; we must pray very hard that the medicine works." Just before he leaves, he leans over and whispers, "Just keep breathing, Naumi, that's all we ask."

Twice in the night, before Jim knows of Naumi's improvement, he wakes up and stares at the ceiling.

Jim Judge is not sure when it happened: maybe one evening while he was feeding THE POOL; maybe it didn't just happen once, but over and over, like the hook in a song. More likely, it is still happening. Whatever the case, Jim is coming to the growing realization that security—real security that doesn't depend on a correct arrangement of circumstances—comes only by not trying to secure it. Rather, it comes by giving of control, of plans, and, above all, of yourself.

Jim began to make some hard realizations. In his focus on finding God's will, he often lost sight of God. In the fear of wasting his life, he may have trashed some opportunities. In his desire to find "it"—that special place of ministry somewhere in the future—he sometimes lost sight of "them"—the people God was placing in his life, day to day.

"I finally had to say that God could do whatever He wanted with my life," Jim says. "The leadings had to be from His perspective and not mine. I had to take them day to day and minute by minute." It was a decision to live in the here and now. For Jim, a person who needed a sense of control, it was a step of trust and obedience.

Remarkable things began to happen in the lives of the Judges. Ministry opportunities began to "open up" at Jim's practice—deep issues involving people whose marriages, finances, and lives were out of control. He began to realize that beneath the glitter and pace of suburbia was a disturbing and hideous core of need, as black as anything that Africa could offer. Nothing less than spiritual cures were demanded.

The Judges also, over a period of time, became aware of the spiritual erosions in their own lives. They both felt the need to be connected, as they once were, with people who were without God, without hope. God led them to a church with a heart for unbelievers where, for the first three or four months, they cried "tears of joy" through each service. They reveled in the excellence, the diversity, the emphasis on spiritual gifts, and the passion for lost people. "These people were living like church was the most important thing in the world," Jim says. Their faith, which was increasingly becoming a lifestyle, was rekindled.

There were other changes, often painful ones. They decided to put their house up for sale. A smaller house, one without THE POOL, would free up energy and time.

In late November of 1989, their minister gave a message about Christians making "a costly gift." The phrase stuck in Jim's mind; he would often wake up at night with it ringing in his ears. About the same time, he heard this from a friend: the Kijabe Medical Center in Kenya had a desperate need for a doctor for a one-year period. Would he be interested in helping out? It would mean pursuing the sale of his house, working without pay, uprooting his wife and three children, and working in a medical center in a country infested with AIDS.

The timing, as it turned out, was perfect.

Dr. Jim Judge is looking for monkeys. On an African hillside as steep as it is green, Jim is standing dead still, gazing up at the trees, trying to follow his oldest daughter's line of sight as she points upward. "I thought I saw something move," she says. Just another false alarm. "Oh well," Jim says, "at least we get a walk through the country." Gives them time, father and daughter, to build a memory.

Another in a series of memories. What started out as an act of obedience and risk has turned out to be one of the best years in the lives of the Judges. They have begun to call it "their furlough" from their ministry in the suburbs of the United States. Above all, they have been able to slow down, to evaluate and to experience. Despite the poverty and disease, Africa has taught them a great deal about the sickness of the suburbs. The people of Africa have taught them lessons about community, beauty, and simple pleasures.

From their backyard, across the Rift Valley, they have watched the night fires on Mount Longonot, orange on black, the annual preparation for the growing season. They have traveled on safaris and seen a single spotted leopard in a tree and thousands of flamingos on a shore, an unearthly white line. They have joined a church service in Gilgal, the little boys beating rhythms on the skins of animals. They have spent a weekend with the Maasai, an ancient African tribe, and a morning at sunrise crossing red-purple waters. They have seen the suffering and the poverty, mothers holding their children in death, and understand what it means to be privileged. They have come to understand, once again, that life is about giving, not getting, and experiencing, not racing. They have learned a new appreciation of God and of each other.

The risks, as it turns out, have been nothing compared to the rewards. "I wanted memories for my kids," Jim says. "I wanted to give them a solid thing that they could look back on and laugh about. I want them to tell their children about their insane father who sold their house, packed everything up in a box, and took them all to Africa for a year. I wanted them to not just hear about their parents' dependence on God but actually give them an example of a dramatic step of faith. I wanted a lab where I could show them God at work and the benefits of faith."

On a steep, green hillside in Africa, Jim and Emily aren't looking for monkeys anymore. The rain has started, followed by a downpour. As they slide down the hill, sometimes feet-first, sometimes head-first, sometimes holding on to one another for support, they are saturated with mud and water. Their laughter, at times, seems out of control.

SERVANTHOOD

6

LOVE THAT'S
FULL OF SURPRISES

"Taking the very nature of a servant."
—*Philippians 2:7*

I didn't really know the man, except for what I read of him. His life ended tragically and ironically. At the time of his death, only 120 pounds stretched along his six-foot-four-inch frame. His entire body was colorless, even his lips. His hair, beard, and nails were hideously long and unkempt. Many of his teeth were rotting, black stumps. A tumor—a reddened stump among a few strands of gray hair—was beginning to emerge from the side of his head. On his arms and thighs and clustered tightly in his groin area were needle marks. He was a junkie, skin-popping more than twenty grams daily, sometimes three or four times that much. His eyes most often looked dead, but occasionally they gleamed from their deep sunken sockets with a surprising and frightening intensity.

This, the man who was the envy of a generation. During his life, he had it all—power, money, fame, unlimited pleasures. He owned strong things and weak people. He gave himself unreservedly to self-indulgence. "If ever a man had what it takes to be satisfied," the jealous public would say, "it had to be Howard Hughes."

I didn't really know the woman, save for the few times I saw her in a small church in Michigan. There was nothing outstanding about her, really. She volunteered in the church kitchen, an elderly woman, average in size and appearance, dressed conservatively. In my mind, she was remarkable in only two ways. First, there was her consistency. Each time I visited the church, she was there, in the kitchen, fogged slightly in my memory by the steam of soup. And then there were her eyes. They gleamed with a surprising kind of depth.

This, a woman noticed by few, envied by no one. If I had to guess, she had little of what the world considers valuable—money, fame, power, or possessions. Judging by her clothes, it would be safe to bet that she owned little and gave much. She lived in the shadow of serving others. "If ever a woman had cause to complain," the world would sigh, "it was this woman." I don't even know her name. But I remember her smile. It spoke of joy.

There are all kinds of people in this world. There are people who like dogs and people who like cats. We affectionately call them dog people and cat people. There are swimming pool people and beach people. Morning people and night people. Coffee people and tea people. The list goes on and on. Humans are immensely diverse with a kaleidoscope of different interests, temperaments, and outlooks.

And yet, in the midst of all the variety, there is a strangely familiar thread that unites us, an interest we all share: self-interest. Regardless of the continent, the political system, the economic status, the race, it is the universal dark side of humanity: the desire for the last piece of pie, the cause for World War III, the angry hunger in our eyes. It is Me First. This ingrained philosophy of life equates happiness with self-indulgence. It is the belief that power, fame, money, and thrills are the tools we can use to measure success.

Today's world celebrates this particular manifestation of depravity. Never before in modern history has the notion of the bloated human had greater acceptance. It is our generation, after all, that has been named the Me Generation. It was the eighties that saw greed elevated to the status of a bug-eyed idol. Fewer and fewer decisions were made on the basis of values, morals, and a sense of justice. Instead, answers came wrapped around appetites. Does this fulfill my needs? Does it satisfy my sexual hunger? Quench my thirst for more? Feed my lust for power? The key adjective was "my." Our role model switched from Mother Teresa to Madonna. The message was clear: indulge, satiate, pursue pleasures without restraint. Selfish interest was not only tolerated, but actively promoted and encouraged. Entire industries, such as advertising and glamour modeling, sprouted in the fertile soul of such unblushing self-centeredness. We have been taught the lesson over and over again: More for me is better for me. The world be damned.

And it has been. The Me First mindset has led our society to the verge of internal collapse. Escapism, perversion, AIDS, unwanted pregnancies, violence, political scandal, and family breakups are all symptoms of our modern-day madness, our obsession with Me.

A LOST NOTION

One way to track the pulse of a society is to measure its words. Their meanings and values change with the times and movements of history. Take the word "servant." Before complaint became a national way of life, it was considered an honor to serve someone. There was no higher cause than to provide for the needs of others out of love. Yet in a culture that panders to self-expression and individualism, "servant" has virtually disappeared from our vocabularies. The six o'clock news features one self-absorbed person after another assertively demanding his or her individual rights. Occasionally a newscast ends with a "human interest" story on someone who serves others. What surprises us is not that this person is featured, but the obvious fact that the servant—one who looks after more than his own self-interest—is now considered a novelty, the odd man out.

We are only gradually awakening to the full extent of the disaster. Those willing to peer through the haze of their selfish pursuits can see the vague outlines of their foundations collapsing. Slowly we are realizing that the things that make life important—our values, our sense of community, our wholeness—are the very things we have been destroying. We "find" ourselves, and much to our surprise, we find ourselves in trouble. We are left reeling, feeling alone, trying to keep our lives from unraveling in the chaos. We discover that pure self-interest is, in the end, self-destructive.

DIVINE LOGIC

Change can come, but only slowly. Deeply ingrained Me First patterns—to say nothing about our sin nature—cannot be broken overnight. It is no surprise that Jesus had to devote tremendous time and effort to teaching His followers a new way of living. It was a curious form of language He used to teach them, almost as if He reversed the common usage of terms: "Mine" became "yours," "getting" became "giving," and "ruler" became "servant."

Jesus' conversations with His disciples became confusing at times, as when two men try to talk to one another in different languages. This was especially true in His interactions with Peter. As hard as he tried, Peter often seemed to hear Jesus wrong. Jesus said "kingdom"; Peter heard "rule." Jesus said "stand firm"; Peter heard "fight." The problem was their conflicting perspectives: the difference between human understanding and divine wisdom.

Mark 8 illustrates this clearly. Jesus has just told His disciples that he would have to suffer and die: He had attacked the power structures, and now He had to pay. Peter took offense. He rebuked the Son of God, telling Him in no uncertain terms that such a course of action would be a waste of wisdom, life, and authority. Surely Jesus would not allow the gospel to end with the disgraceful footnote of a gravestone.

This dialogue reveals Peter as a courageous man: It is no small matter to confront the Son of God. But his courage, as Jesus well knew, was fueled less by strength of character than by passion and ignorance. Imagine Peter, a two-bit fisherman netting a meager livelihood in the Sea of Galilee. High on energy, but low on dreams. By temperament, driven, but for what? And then along came Jesus. Suddenly Peter's world— his life—was transformed. Finally he had a purpose as large as his passion. This was, after all, no minor league player Peter had hooked up with. This was God Himself. No longer was Peter fishing in a small pond. He was the right-hand man of a miracle worker, a radical, a revolutionary. Peter was absolutely certain he had attached his star to a man who would change the world. Peter didn't know for sure how Jesus would do it, but he was sure that Jesus had a grand plan—and equally sure that a premature death was *not* part of it. Such talk was nonsense. Someone *had* to get Jesus back on track.

Jesus' reaction must have taken Peter by surprise. His words struck quickly, with a fire that seared Peter's heart: He called him Satan, the very enemy himself. In Jesus' words one senses both frustration and fatigue. For years Jesus had tried to teach His disciples that the Me First attitude was not the path to life.

"I have come to serve," He told them over and over again. "I have not come to tug the strings of power or reduce others to puppets for a cause, but to give myself away." His whole life was a display of servanthood, selflessness, and love. His death was to be the ultimate example of loving others, and He wanted His disciples to understand, especially Peter, His right-hand man.

But Peter, like the others and like ourselves, was still focused on his own agenda. He wanted what Jesus wanted as long as it didn't cost him his Me First mindset. Despite Jesus' efforts, Peter was still rooted to the world's value system of power, promotion, and privilege. When Jesus said He had to die in order to serve others, Peter didn't care one whit about God's redemptive plan. He could only feel the pain in his heart, the drain of losing his purpose and his Friend in one swift blow. His interests, not God's, were at the center of his concern.

Peter's actions demonstrate the tenacity of the Me First mindset. It is not a mere relational virus, a slight psychological maladjustment, or a hand-me-down from imperfect parenting. You can't take a pill for it, or work it out in counseling, or escape it through biofeedback. Jesus told us it is a disease from hell, deeply rooted in the human heart. Without radical measures, it will drain the fulfillment from our lives and cost us our souls for eternity.

And the only measure radical enough is death. Death to self. The Me First mindset must be crucified. If anyone wishes to come after me, Jesus stated again and again, he must deny himself, pick up his cross, and lose his life. What does such a death mean? That we give our lives away voluntarily in love and service to God and others.

But at this point there's a twist, a spin of logic, another divine paradox. This dying to self—this giving, this servanthood—lands us smack dab in the middle of the very thing we want most: deep personal satisfaction. The first to give me this radical information was one of my college professors. "Fulfillment," he would say in a thick French accent, "will never come through self-gratification." I can remember sitting in his classroom, breaking out in a cold sweat. His words contradicted everything I had previously learned. "If you really want to live, then give yourself to God and others. Devote yourself to faithful and humble service, and you will discover joy."

PAY ATTENTION, PETER!

It is a message we are slow to get. Peter and the other disciples never quite understood it until Jesus was dead. But that didn't keep Jesus from pounding home His favorite theme. In fact, during His last meal with His disciples, He taught perhaps His greatest object lesson on the importance of serving others in love. The central characters in the drama are, once again, Jesus and Peter. The setting is the Upper Room where Jesus gathers the disciples to share the Passover supper. One by one the disciples flow into the Upper Room. Each one notices that no one is at the door to wash their dirty feet, as was the custom of the time. Dirty feet and low tables were a bad combination; any self-respecting person who threw a dinner party would have a rank-and-file servant on hand to perform the task. As the disciples enter, they wonder what to do. Who will wash their feet? Why didn't Jesus arrange to have one of the women followers do it? Not one of them is willing to condescend to the task. Perhaps it never entered their minds.

At any rate, they finally sit down at the table, feet unwashed. As the evening meal is served, a discussion breaks out as to which of them is the greatest. Jesus' heart breaks. His closest followers argue about greatness with dirty feet. They seek honor without earning it. Is there no one, He wonders, who will serve a brother? Is the love they have learned so short-sighted and ungiving?

As Jesus removes His robe and puts on a servant's towel, what does He feel? Agony, regret, sorrow? Does He wash His disciples' feet with His tears? Jesus had spent His entire ministry trying to develop in them attitudes of humility and servanthood and now, at this final gathering before His death, no one is willing to perform the smallest act of love. They argue about greatness and seem to have no idea what it means.

Jesus moves from one disciple to the next, washing and drying their feet. Finally He begins to wash Peter's feet. There are, as expected, sparks of misunderstanding. Peter, in a dither, says, "No, Jesus, you will never wash my feet." He deplores the idea that the Son of God would ever have to stoop that low. Jesus' answer stresses once again the importance of servanthood: "Unless I wash you, you have no part with me." To which Peter, in his typical extremist fashion, responds, "Then wash all of me."

Oh, Peter. I can imagine Jesus grabbing him by the shoulders and shaking him. "Pay attention, Peter. Listen—really listen this time—to what I'm trying to tell you. Look at My hands, Peter. Watch what they are doing. Let the meaning of this lesson seep into every pore of your skin and touch your heart with understanding. Unless you grasp the meaning of this lesson, you cannot be My follower; you will play no part in My redemptive plan. You must learn to be a servant, Peter. A servant."

Jesus must have wondered what He had to do to get the point across to His followers. What would bring them to the point of action? How far must He go to demonstrate servanthood? His next actions revealed just how far He was willing to go. He took the bread and broke it, saying, "This is My body that is broken for you." And then He picked up the wine and said, "This is My blood that is spilled for you."

In a few hours, in His ultimate act of servanthood, He would die on the cross. The nails, He hoped, would drive home His point.

Profile:
Angie Garber

7

ANGIE GARBER:
EIGHTY YEARS OLD
AND ON A
NAVAJO RESERVATION

*"You don't even feel like you are being a servant
to someone, if you love them."*

—*Angie Garber*

*B*ehind Angie Garber's house, just beyond the playground of the Brethren Navajo Mission in New Mexico, there is a cemetery. In the middle of a wasteland, the flowers there catch your eye. It's not so much the surprise—the unexpected stabs of color in brown dirt—but, more, the sense of progression.

Near the front of the cemetery, the soil recently turned, there is a certain beauty: someone's sad and bright garden. Deeper, a few decades in, the brilliance fades—the flowers are fewer, mostly plastic, and the graves less distinct. At some point there are only hints: a splintered cross, a letter or two on a broken stone, a flower's corpse. The fusion is subtle and delicate, yet undeniable. Tombs, flowers, memories—all fading, dust to dust.

Just yesterday, they buried another Navajo here. Angie knows; she can always hear the hopeless wailing. This land, the sacred ground of the Navajos, shows no mercy.

It is a morning approaching Christmas. Angie Garber is in her blue Datsun "L'il Rambler" pick-up truck cutting a gray-orange plume through the desert. She is, she says, doing what she loves best. In between pointing out the homes of the Navajos, many of whom still live in hogans (homes made of mud, clay, and logs), she is singing. *This world, This world is not my home; This world is not my resting place . . .* She interrupts her song, pointing a finger to the horizon. "That's where an old medicine man lives," she says. "He wants me to come over sometime and compare stories."

Angie Garber, nearing the age of eighty, is a woman with many stories. The daughter of an Iowa farmer, she stayed at home to take care of her mentally unstable mother until late in her life. Instead of going to college, she says, she got polio. She has never been married. At the age of thirty-eight, while attending a seminary in Indiana, she was asked to teach at a mission on an Indian reservation in New Mexico. Because she had nothing else to do, and she had read James Fenimore Cooper as a child, she decided to go.

For more than four decades, she has lived in a tiny off-white home with three rooms: a combination kitchen and living room (not big enough for a couch), a bedroom just barely big enough for a single bed, and a bathroom. She has a Norge deluxe refrigerator that sounds like a small Piper Cub.

She has her luxuries, she says. A small organ to play hymns, a portable AM-FM radio with a cracked speaker to hear J. Vernon McGee and, in her front yard, a small cement pond with goldfish. In honor of forty years of service at the reservation, she was just recently given a television, the first she has owned.

Her focus in life has never been on things. "I don't want to just have things," she says. "When you love things, you use people. I don't care about getting things for my house. I've got enough, more than enough. The Bible says with food and raiment be satisfied." And, she adds with a laugh, a little gas for her pickup truck thrown in on the side.

She is, for the most part, isolated from the world. The nearest hint of civilization is the town of Cuba, a narrow, bony village that clings to Interstate 44 some thirty miles from the mission. There is a gas station there that gives away free showers with every fill-up.

As her pickup moves on dirt roads past twisted junipers and gnarly, half-starved piñons, she is not complaining. There's an occasional flare of arthritis and, every once in a while, her back "goes out" on her, but nothing serious.

But Angie is not without her concerns, for example, the mud blocking the road in front of her. "There's a woman who lives back there that I haven't seen for a while," she says, gunning the engine of her pickup. "I want to make sure she's all right." Throwing mud, Angie quickly slips into another story, this one involving a joke about Navajos who live on the moon. "When the white men come," the punch line goes, "don't give them any land."

Angie has that sort of laugh. Contagious, rolling with her words, and, at its center, touched with inflections of heartache. It is no easy life God has chosen for her. And she, a woman who wears frilly bonnets and cries during hymns, is no weak-kneed sister. Almost by necessity, she is a woman of character: She chases dogs with brooms, starts her pickup by popping the clutch, and clings tightly to her opinions.

"When I first came here to serve," she says, "I thought this was the most desolate place in the world. I called it a desert."

Now, her pickup freshly spattered with mud, she calls it an oasis. The woman she has come to see, widowed and alone, is doing fine. She runs toward Angie, hugs her, and calls her a sister in Christ.

By a fire, Angie sits in a hogan, reading from the Bible in Navajo: an ancient, metrical, almost hypnotic rhythm fills the room. It is the Christmas story.

Angie has stopped by with some food and clothes. Outside the wind stings, gritty with snow and sand, and whines inside cracks in the walls. Inside a baby cries and a Panasonic radio pulsates with the voice of the world. Something about the glory of love.

There is not much to this one-room house: a table (a board supported by milk crates), a bed (a cot with a mat and broken springs), scattered skillets and clothes, and a small, limping brown dog. Above it all, a calendar from Montoya's Dry Goods with a picture of a snow-covered mountain: all in blue, peaceful and perfect.

As Angie stops her reading to try and quiet the baby, a Navajo woman, a face as etched as the land, sits listening, quietly holding a bad heart. Her husband, sitting nearby, reads a pamphlet, some kind of cartoon, tilting back almost comically in his chair. Angie has been here before. She knows that the family is not really interested in what she has to say.

Barring some miraculous change, the woman will die soon and her husband will be left, hopeless, to raise their children.

If Angie has learned anything, it is that this is a harsh and often hopeless land. And it is the land itself, perhaps, that provides the roots for understanding the Navajo. At first glance, the land is a wasteland: thirsty, never tamed, and bone-level lonely. But deeper, etched in the ancestral tombs and in the sudden storms that sweep the desert with fire and rain, there is mystery, a sense of what can only remain unspoken. Says Angie: "There is something about this land that attracts you, holds you."

Ask a Navajo why he or she stays on the reservation and the reply will almost always be: "We are Indians; we are Navajos. This is our land." They have lived here forever.

For the Navajo, the land is considered sacred, the very gift of God. The land, however, offers precious little. There are few jobs available. Most Navajos receive assistance from the United States government to live.

It is a land caught between two worlds and a volatile set of paradoxes: a cling to history and a need for a future, pride and debilitating circumstances, independence and subjection. Gentle by nature, the Navajo lives in an uneasy world of turmoil and boredom. There has been a gradual seeping of the "world" into the Navajo community while traditional values, slowly ebbing, remain strong. These conflicts have created vacuums and a loss of identity. Drinking and drug abuse on the reservation are at epidemic levels. Many religions—everything from the Jehovah's Witnesses to the Peyote drug cult—have infiltrated. In the confusion of competing values, truth has become difficult to discern.

Even love has its limits. Servanthood, Angie says, carries no guarantees. During her decades at the reservation, Angie has seen comparatively few people develop life-changing relationships with Jesus Christ. Three small churches have been established but, even on such holy ground, it is almost impossible to tell sincere faith from empty words. Says Angie: "I don't think anyone *really* knows how many genuine converts there are."

In such an environment, Angie has learned that personal value and purpose must flow exclusively from a relationship with Jesus Christ. "You have to keep your eyes on the Lord, you just can't start looking around. Your joy has to come from the Lord. The issue is not how many people come to know the Lord or not; the main thing is: Is your heart for the Lord? If you didn't love the Lord, you couldn't work or serve here."

Love, she has learned, is not really love unless it is unconditional. It must flow out of gratitude, and not personal need. Love requires a great deal, precisely everything.

That is why nearly every morning for more than thirty years—broken only by the roads being washed out or her back being thrown out—she has climbed into her L'il Rambler pickup truck, popped the clutch, and made her "rounds" to people she has come to love. She no longer considers herself a missionary to these people. She would rather be called their friend.

"I have been out here long enough," says Angie, "to talk to the children about their grandparents. They know I mean to stick around. If you are here a long time, you have shared their heartaches and their joys. You share life together."

If it sounds quaint, eternal, or noble, that's the wrong idea. Mostly, it's routine, casual, or painful. Today Angie drives past a house in shambles. She tells the story of a little Navajo boy, whom she taught during her first years at the reservation. The boy, if she dare make such a claim, was one of her favorites. He was small and frail and clung to Angie. Early on, he claimed to know the Lord. Angie continued a relationship with him through school, his marriage, and his first child. Then his wife started drinking and eventually died in a drunken stupor. Overwhelmed with the loss of his wife, the young man started to drink and has yet to stop. He lives with another woman.

Angie could tell story after story. Love involves sorrow. "The only heart that can love," she says, "is one that is broken. You wouldn't have much love if you couldn't share the heartaches."

But love, despite the pain, is the only thing Angie has found worth committing her life to. "Christ says to love," Angie says. "That's the great thing that He wants you to do. If you love somebody, then you are going to be a blessing to them. You don't even feel like you are being a servant to someone, if you love them. It's really important to care about them, and to *show* them that you care about them. Then they will listen to you, they'll hear you."

There's at least one other thing about love, Angie says. Love, that is, poured out as a sacrifice. It is full of surprises.

"You get so much of a reward," Angie says, jumping from the seat of her pickup truck still another time. "When you love others, people take you in as one of their own. You always feel special when you are loved. The best thing about love is that you know the Lord is working in you. People don't love you for how wonderful you are; they love you because you belong to the Lord. They can see Him in you."

Angie, hunched over against a cold wind and from many years, makes her way through a fence into a garden. Against a low black sky, a man named Ben, his face veiled in the shadow of a wide-brimmed hat, is working the frozen ground. Spring is just months away. If there is one thing the Navajo knows well it is the land; a proper garden depends upon preparation.

Together, they retreat into a porch filled with his collections: dried flowers, bones, and rocks . . . things that mean a lot to him, ancient reminders. As a teakettle whines in the distance, Angie begins reading from her Navajo Bible. She stops in the middle of one verse and comments: "It says that Jesus is the one who came down. Did you ever stop and think about what that means?" The man nods and Angie continues: "We can't really understand what it means that Jesus came down and showed His love for us."

Ben is old; his face is etched by the weather of sorrow, the seeds of character. He smiles slightly. His life, Angie says, has been transformed by the love of God. Just a few years ago, after doing time in prison for killing his wife, he came into a personal relationship with Jesus Christ.

"I can't understand that kind of love," Ben says, shaking his head. Angie, as she has done for more than four decades in this desert wasteland, continues on in the Word of God.

HUMILITY

8

THE PECKING
ORDER

"He humbled himself."

—*Philippians 2:8*

*T*ake ten chickens. Any ten. Put them in a pen together, and spread a little chicken feed. In short order,
you will witness an amazing phenomenon. In a matter
of minutes, the chickens, previously strangers, will
form a hierarchy based on dominance; or, in everyday
language, they will establish a Pecking Order. Instinc-
tively, they will determine, through a series of skir-
mishes, who the Number One Chicken will be; then the
Number Two; the Number Three; all the way down to
the unlucky Number Ten Chicken.

Much is at stake in this dance of domination.
Chicken Number One pecks at and intimidates
Chicken Number Two, without experiencing any kind

of retribution from Chicken Number Two. Chicken Number Two will take it from Chicken Number One but will turn around and peck away at Chicken Number Three, who will, in turn, take out its frustration on Chicken Number Four. The Pecking Order continues all the way down to Chicken Number Ten, who, needless to say, has a pretty miserable life: pecked, but no one to peck.

Recently I was invited to an appreciation luncheon for the president of a bank. It's not something I normally do, but this man had been attending our church for several months and I welcomed the opportunity to get to know him better. As I got out of my car, I congratulated myself for remembering to bring a sport coat. But that sense of pride was shortlived. Every other man in the banquet room wore full formal garb: dark suits, starched white shirts, gold cuff links, and red ties. When the butter was passed, it could have been a Rolex commercial.

I was seated at a table with nine other men, all guests of the bank and strangers to me. Quickly a conversation began. The discussion, for the most part, focused on the following issues: *where* we worked, *how much* our company made, and *how many* people worked for us. In a sense, we were scratching the ground, flaring our feathers. It made little difference that the ground was not dirt but plush carpet, and instead of feathers, there was the parading of power suits and the flashing of carats. There was no doubt about it: We were checking each other out, strutting and clucking, trying to figure out where each one of us stood. The Pecking Order.

Twenty minutes later, dressed in my sport coat and Timex watch, I felt certain I knew my place. It didn't take an Einstein to figure out who was Chicken Number Ten.

It would be tempting to dismiss the event as an anomaly, to claim that the Pecking Order belongs to an exclusive few. But you and I know better than that. This kind of thing happens everywhere: at sporting events, parties, class reunions, family picnics. Church. At a recent lunch at a conference for pastors, most of the discussion revolved around three questions: *How many* people attend your church? *How big* is your budget? *How large* is your staff? Even pastors try to establish a Pecking Order. No one, in fact, is immune to the sickness. Nearly all of us look at other people's professions, educations, wardrobes, cars, homes, and try to figure out where they fit in the Pecking Order. We measure each other by counting carefully.

It may seem harmless. "It's an innocent little game," you say. "What does it matter?" But it does matter. There is something involved here that runs deep in every human heart, and has nothing to do with innocence. This is no little mind game. For most of us, subconsciously developing a Pecking Order and figuring out where we fit into it is serious—and dangerous—business, which radically affects how we relate to others. For each of us, the natural tendency is to treat those above us on the Pecking Order with admiration, cordiality, and honor (even though we may secretly envy or even despise them). Those below us, we tend to treat with insensitivity, callousness, or even contempt.

It's understandable. Pecking Orders provide some order in our lives. In a world filled with chaos, there is a sense of comfort in knowing where we fit. When we know the structure, we know when and where to choose our fights. We know when a peck is to be accepted—the pain swallowed with quiet dignity—and when we should exercise our rights and peck back with slightly greater force.

We find labels convenient, for they provide us with clues: white collar/blue collar; management/labor; middle class/lower class; college graduate/high school dropout. We listen for titles and numbers and other tip-offs. We look for jewelry and hood ornaments and designer clothes. This information helps us peg other people—and ourselves. Once we know the Pecking Order, we know what is expected of us.

IT SIMPLY IS

In its most dramatic form, the Pecking Order is a sight to behold. I was speaking at a conference recently and saw Martina Navratilova walk into the hotel where the conference was being held. You should have seen the doors fly open in front of her, the elevator lines allowing her cuts, the restaurant host seating her immediately.

Several years ago, my wife and I attended a dinner where the guest of honor was Henry Kissinger. It was amazing to see the respect the man commanded. When he grabbed a roll, there were hands diving for the butter dish, vying for the favor of passing it to him.

That kind of behavior seems instinctive. Navratilova and Kissinger are branded by the Pecking Order as "important people." It's natural that we pay them respect. That's just the way it works. When the president of the company asks for a favor, he'll get it. When the VIP, the owner, or the superstar comes around we reflexively treat them preferentially. It takes little more than a snap of a finger for us to jump into action.

But what happens when the janitor at our company wants five minutes of our time? Or the single mom next door asks for a small favor, again? Or the teenager who mows our lawn requests our advice? How do we react? Depends on our mood, maybe, or how many times we have been asked before. The Pecking Order give us that kind of flexibility. People who are "below us" professionally, monetarily, fashionwise, housewise, talentwise, whatever . . . we yawn and say, "It's *only* you." Honor is optional. We show interest only if we are so moved. We often make calculations in our minds: will this be worth my time, money or effort?

That is just how the system works. The Pecking Order doesn't pretend to be without prejudice; it doesn't bother itself with questions of right or wrong. It simply is. Like a ruler with unquestioned authority, the Pecking Order doesn't concern itself with alternatives. If you want to live in this world, then you have to live by its rules. For good or bad, that's just the way the system works.

PRETENTION VERSUS HUMILITY

In all of history, no one was a more qualified candidate for the Pecking Order than Jesus Christ. Think about it. He owned and created *everything* and *everybody.* All Rolexes, all Porsches, all CEOs and rock bands, all mansions, all power and authority, all wisdom. He could have chosen any career—business, politics, sports, medicine—and have been a major player. He had the Right Stuff. The Pecking Order was His for the taking—the Number One of all Number Ones, the quintessential King of the Hill.

But Jesus Christ hated the Pecking Order. In fact, He spent His entire ministry ripping at its foundations. He seized every opportunity to turn the Pecking Order upside down and inside out. Those who had reached the top—the religious leaders of Israel—He often scorched with His words. He called them hypocrites, white-washed tombs, snakes. He accused them of robbing widows, being filled with dead men's bones, and in so many words, worshiping themselves. In a nation subjected to another political power and lacking superstars, the religious leaders were, perhaps, the most important, powerful, and respected people in Israel—the VIPs—worthy, they believed, of great honor. Yet Jesus scorned them. He spurned the Pecking Order.

The problem, Jesus said, was one of focus. The religious leaders focused on externals—how they appeared to others on the outside. That's why they loved their impressive rituals of prayer. And their season tickets to the best seats in the synagogue. That's why they loved their Neiman Marcus robes, and the way the common people looked at them. By building a mountain of externals, they formed a wall of separation. They used their titles and tassels as visible reminders that, in the scheme of things, there was a difference between "us" and "them." And, clearly, us was better than them. They viewed life from a perspective of pretension.

It is no surprise that when Jesus and the religious leaders met, the sparks flew. Jesus had no need for externals. He had, in fact, voluntarily stripped Himself of all of them: His titles as owner and creator, His position at the right hand of the throne of God, and the honor of receiving the praise of the cosmos. For the sake of love, and to break down walls of separation, Jesus shed Himself of externals, and became as unpretentious as a naked baby born in a stable.

Jesus' perspective was shaped by a deep sense of humility. It was a humility where none was called for; Jesus, as God, clearly deserved His titles, position, and praise. But as we have seen, Jesus "did not consider equality with God something to be grasped." He wanted, instead, to relate with man on an equal level. Where the religious leaders of His day relished the separation between themselves and "the common people," Jesus sought to break down the barriers, even those imposed by His divine rights. Humility was at the core of His philosophy. More times than not, He used His power for the powerless, showed love to the loveless, and served those who could not possibly return the favor. With characteristic consistency He repeatedly rejected a Pecking Order based on conditional response.

EVEN IN OUR WORLD

The Pecking Order, Jesus said with His life, words and actions, is not only inherently flawed, but, in some ways, a working definition of evil. Through humility, He sought to throw a wrench into the whole depraved system. If we read the Gospels carefully, we can almost see Jesus *looking* for opportunities to make trouble. He would say: "You will be great in My sight when you demonstrate servanthood to the least of these around you. You will be great in My sight when you serve, honor, and respect the lowest of the low." He would talk about visiting those in prison, inviting orphans and widows to banquets, caring for the elderly, the blind, and the sick. And then He would back up His words with action: healing lepers, feeding the hungry, and throwing parties for, in contemporary language, "the scum of the earth." He loved the worst of sinners.

His focus, more times than not, was on Chickens Eight, Nine, and Ten. In so doing, Jesus ripped across the grain of the world's value system. He was, without question, the most countercultural man ever to live on the face of the earth. He rebelled against the very system that provided order on the planet. Jesus painfully demonstrated that love was a real possibility, even in a world soaked with sin and prejudice.

The real shocker is that Jesus asks us, today, to be as countercultural and rebellious as He was. Into our screwed-up, twisted, dog-eat-dog world, He wants us to bring humility and servanthood. They will know you are My followers, He said, if you love one another. He didn't include a footnote or a loophole that limits our responsibility to those above us on the Pecking Order. He said to love one another. Period. With no qualifiers attached.

It was no small command.

SO MUCH FOR PRIDE AND PREJUDICE

In Philippians 2:3, Paul writes, "Do nothing out of selfish ambition or vain conceit, but in humility consider others better than yourselves." The phrase "in humility" is critical, for it provides an undergirding philosophy. It is the same point from which Jesus began His incarnation: "He humbled himself." If Jesus, the Son of God, chose the path of humility, how much more should we? Jesus had no reason for humility; we have every reason for it.

Humility is important for another critical reason. The Pecking Order, at its very skeleton, is built on pride and prejudice, on the belief that some of us are better than others. Humility is the wisdom to know that each of us, in the eyes of God, is the same: deeply flawed, yet precious. None of us, regardless of our titles and possessions, is worthy of more than hell. None of us can climb ourselves into a state of grace. God's redeeming mercy is, by definition, totally undeserved. Yet it is offered freely to all. Christ's blood was shed for Jeffrey Dahmer, Adolph Hitler, Mother Teresa, and me and you.

Such ideas are the roots of humility. God offered us His love without considering whether we deserved it or not; we are called to offer love in exactly the same way. Or, in the words of Paul, "in humility consider others more important than yourselves." Can you think of any idea more opposed to the Pecking Order? Can you imagine the implications of actually applying that notion to real life?

A COSTLY REVOLUTION

The implications are staggering. Think about society. Can you imagine what would happen in the marketplace if everybody in the company treated everybody else like a VIP? If officers treated clerical workers the same; if presidents showed honor and respect to night janitors? Imagine a political system where politicians really cared about the people they governed. And what could happen to our educational system if all teachers really worked for the welfare of their students?

Think about our marriages. What if a husband stopped viewing himself as "Chicken Number One," who has the right to peck away at his wife, "Chicken Number Two," who, in retaliation, pecks at the kids, the dog, or a door-to-door salesman.

Can you imagine what would happen if each husband said, "My wife is a Very Important Person, and I am going to honor, respect and encourage her." And if the wife said the same thing about her husband?

Love like that can mark people for the rest of their lives. There is, if nothing else, the impact of surprise, the uplifting jolt of having someone considered higher up on the Pecking Order treat you preferentially. My brother recently went to a college football game. At half-time, he stood near the tunnel where the players enter the playing field. Gathered at the end of the tunnel was a group of small boys wanting to get a better look at their heroes. As the players emerged, they all ran past, except for one player, Mark Messner, an outstanding linebacker from Michigan. Mark stopped dead in his tracks for an instant, then walked deliberately toward a boy standing off to the side. Gently he picked him up, hugged him, and said a few words before he returned to the field. Can you imagine the impact?

That's one isolated incident. Imagine the impact we could leave on people's lives if we all practiced preferential treatment for everyone? Imagine how we could please God if we went out of our way to show His love to those less fortunate, less privileged, or less powerful than we? Imagine the relational and spiritual revolutions that could occur. But it will never happen unless we make it happen. It's easy to say, "I'll start doing that when I have more time," or "after I get my promotion," or "when I see others doing the same thing." But love doesn't run on excuses. Change comes only with willful movement. Impact follows on the heels of action.

But let's not be quick to ignore reality. Such behavior, though potentially revolutionary, carries a cost. You don't buck something as powerful as the Pecking Order without getting bucked back. Anyone who loves, really loves, learns the pain of rejection, hatred, and anger. Some people, especially those the system treats with favor, do not take well to the concept of unconditional love. Paul learned that. He paid a heavy price for authoring the words about humility we have just looked at. During the course of his life, he was beaten, whipped, imprisoned, abandoned, betrayed. And, finally, martyred.

Or consider the life of Jesus Christ. Emptying Himself of His divine right, He humbly descended to earth. With every breath, every word, every action, He defied the Pecking Order. He loved unconditionally. And He ended up high on a hill outside of Jerusalem, hated by the elite, crucified by a system He came to destroy, a ragged sign placed over His blood-streaked head. King of the Hill.

That's where love got Him.

Profile:
Mike Singletary

9

MIKE SINGLETARY:
IN THE MIDDLE
OF THE CHAOS

"I was trapped within myself. I had pride and I thought that was strength, but it was actually weakness. I became totally defeated within myself. I did not trust and I did not believe in myself at all, and I did not see why anyone else would believe in me either."

— *Mike Singletary*

*S*hortly after winning the 1986 Super Bowl, Mike Singletary became afraid of the dark. This is no joke: He slept with a light on.

Fear, in fact, overwhelmed his life. This was Mike Singletary, all right, the Chicago Bear who has been named to nine Pro Bowls, the one who has earned the nickname, Samurai, the middle linebacking lunatic with The Eyes. Not a man you would expect to be cowering anywhere, anyplace, anytime. But there he was, night after night, broken by the darkness, the quiet.

It was the fear of The Game that had broken him. Not football, mind you; he had proved himself, against long odds, to be one of the best. Defensive Player of the Year, in fact. It was a much more subtle and dangerous game that he feared, where the opponent was himself: fierce, deceitful, and full of pride. "I really believed I was going to die," he says.

Singletary met Singletary, and he didn't know what was real. On the one hand, there was Mike Singletary, the Christian: saying the right stuff, athlete-star, near to God, putting on the shiny bright lies. And then there was Mike Singletary, the man in the mirror: muscled and puny, celebrated and pitiful. It was the funhouse mirror: Singletary—the real one, that is—not living up to his image.

Sin distorts. Singletary learned that. And there was sin to deal with: the pride of believing that his accomplishments were his own, the web of hypocrisy, the damage of seeking to live life on his own terms. There was this, specifically: During their engagement, he had been unfaithful to his wife. As bad as that was—and the guilt was nearly eating him alive—he knew that was not the worst of it. He had, through his facade, betrayed his God. "I wanted to be a Christian on my own terms," Singletary says. "Everything had to go my way because I deserved it. That's how I thought."

He knew he had to do something. But there was only this: a huge brick wall. Challenge did not intimidate Singletary, never has. It was more the inevitable ending: Mike Singletary, stripped of pride, would have to lose himself.

Off-season has a curious ring to it, a twisting of the natural, like life comes in manageable terms: some time is more important than others. Glory or value or success is measured only in certain months. Not with Mike Singletary. It is 6 A.M. on a Tuesday in April. He is up, at a table in his dining room, reading Exodus, chapter 29: "For seven days make atonement for the altar and consecrate it. Then the altar will be most holy, and whatever touches it will be holy." A lesson of consistency. He is surrounded with books that ring of a gutsy optimism: You Can Become the Person You Want to Be. Power for Living. A few minutes later, his trainer/therapist arrives. Together they retreat to his basement, to a room that looks like a health club. They chat about the banquet—"the best one yet"—and Singletary concludes, "Big Al was really bringing the Word."

The sweat begins. Today, he is working on the upper body, major muscle groups: lat shrugs, pull-ups, bench, rotation for rotator cups, lower abs, and reverse torso curls. From station to station, eight sets, three hours, building the weight. There is quick, almost barking, conversation.

Bench press. "How many?"

"Three." Add more weight. "Give me one."

"Easy money."

Next station, medicine ball tucked underneath legs. "Up, side-to-side. Slide down a little, you're pulling with your elbows. That's it, perfect."

Next station. Music slams from a corner jam box: *He delivered me.* On a chair is the day's sports page: *Bears Get Hope, Choose Ohio State Defensive End Alonzo Spellman.* Big and talented, undeveloped potential.

"Hold it double this time, Mike . . . 5-6-7-8. That's plenty."

"No, I've got to do more." For Singletary, this is survival. Working hard—harder than all the others—has been his ticket to success. He has always been faced with at least one too many obstacles. Born in a poor neighborhood of Houston, the last of 10 children, his mother was advised to abort him. His parents divorced when he was 12. Suffering from significant hearing loss (either from birth or as a result of working heavy construction with his father), he often stuttered.

Back to the bench press. More weight. "Give me two." Another dime. "Give me one." Next station. "Bring it back up. Come on, push it."

He was told early that he would never make it in football. Too small. He discovered, beyond the physical talent, his heart and mind. He fell in love with obsession. He devoured positive thinking books. Know what you want. Find out what it takes. Study, set goals, work, work, work. Focus. Don't listen to any advice containing the word "can't." Dreams were his ticket out.

There is sweat dripping off Singletary's chin. He pays attention to the details of form. "Don't let your head drop. Bring it up. . . . One more."

He earned a football scholarship at Baylor University. He was told he would have to wait to play. Deep at linebacker. Too small, really. Eight games into the season, he was starting. His sophomore, junior, and senior years, he was defensive player of the league.

"This will be your toughest one, Mike. . . . Give me three." More weight. "One more."

The Chicago Bears swapped second-round picks to draft Singletary. Despite a brilliant collegiate career, there were some reservations. Six feet on tiptoes; 220 pounds wet. Hardly the measurements of a great middle linebacker. How do you weigh the size of the heart? And now, 11 years into his career, 9 straight Pro Bowls, Defensive Player of the Year, NFL Man of the Year, more than 150 starts, 1,300 tackles, 800 solo stops, and only missed 2 starts his entire career.

Next station. More reps. Grunting, pain. "Did you hear something pop?" he asks. The trainer nods no. "Well, it wasn't me." He joins with the music of Alabama in the background, "I might be a memory before too long," he sings, wiping the sweat from his forehead.

Singletary knows he has passed his prime. Slower reflexes, aging, an old man by football standards. But that doesn't mean that he won't be at the top of his game. Greatness will just demand a bit more.

"One more. Push it."

———————

There was at least one problem with Mike Singletary's climb to greatness. He became proud. Given the obstacles, it is understandable if he began to confuse gift with tenacity. "I think I had to develop a no-matter-what-you-say-or-do-I'm-going-to-do-it-this-way attitude," Singletary says. "There was nothing anyone could say or do that could stop me. I think that is where the pride came in." Given the success, it is clear that Singletary became a victim of his own propaganda. He believed that he could do anything: own a multimillion dollar business, star in the movies, write a book. Anything.

He had even found a way to influence the God of the Universe. He had convinced himself that he was doing all he was doing for God. And that God should be mighty glad. In a distorted way, he began to feel that he had earned some slack from God. He could always cut a deal. Because he was Mike Singletary, the man of impossible accomplishments, he deserved special consideration. There were certain things that he needed to stay alive.

He was headed for brokenness. He lived an inconsistent life, and that was not consistent with his personality. In some areas, he would talk God and do whatever he pleased. The sins piled up; the guilt bore in on him like a three hundred-pound fullback at full speed. Out of control, he could see the brick wall approaching. Judging by every external circumstance, he was firmly in control, much to be admired. His team had just won the Super Bowl. He was named Defensive Player of the League. He had money. He was expecting his first child. With determination and a positive attitude, he had shattered every impossible obstacle. And he was slowly falling apart.

The Super Bowl, which should have been the culmination of all he had worked so diligently for, marked the lowest point in his life. "No matter how much I tried to get into it, to get excited about it," he says, "I just couldn't. It was just another game for me." The months that followed were filled with fear. He couldn't sleep. He couldn't eat. He couldn't stand the darkness. The quiet screamed accusations. "I was a mess," he says.

The immediate problem was his relationship with his wife, Kim. Although he had been faithful to her since their marriage, he felt the weight of his sin against her during their engagement. He knew that he had to deal with it, confess to her, and feel her pain. As difficult as that was, there was even a deeper issue: Mike's relationship with God. His unfaithfulness to his Creator burned a hole in his soul. His pride, as great as it was, could not cross the ever-widening chasm. Increasingly he felt the vacuum between what he said he was, and what he actually was. In order to be used by God, his pride would have to be smashed against the wall.

It was then that the realization hit. "It was not who I was that mattered," Singletary says, "but who God is." Singletary began to see that he had confused survival with independence. Given the obstacles, he thought that he could only depend upon himself. He had to stay in control. And it worked. With each year that passed, he became more and more successful against longer and longer odds. If anyone had a right to be proud, to feel self-assured, it was Mike Singletary. But a curious thing began to happen. With his self dependence, he began to feel less confident. "I was trapped within myself," he says. "I had pride and I thought that was strength, but it was actually weakness. I became totally defeated within myself. I did not trust and I did not believe in myself at all, and I did not see why anyone else would believe in me either. When I was by myself, alone, I was afraid."

The late evening light reflects maroon-salmon, a color of May, off the glass towers of the Chicago Hyatt-Regency. Inside, in the Grand Ballroom, with its mandatory crystal stalagmites and peacock napkins, there is an awards ceremony under way. More than five hundred members of the Management Association of Illinois are gathered to honor their best. There are the stiff electronic announcements, the hoots of recognition, the thunder static of claps. With slow and deliberate enunciation, "The Award of Excellence. When I call your name, I'll ask you to come forward and receive your award from our chairman. From the Barnett Company, Jacqueline A. Fickle, also from the Barnett Company, Wilma Sturgill . . . "

For those who belong, it is an important event. For outsiders, especially on this evening when spring clouds roll, breaking in purples, it moves toward monotony. Mike Singletary is here. He seems foreign, yet comfortable, in a black suit, white shirt, and color-splashed tie. As the awards ceremony comes to an end, the keynote speaker is introduced. Singletary rises and speaks with passion.

The system, he says, is falling apart. Greed and self-indulgence are eating at the values that once made America great. Many people are focused on feeding their egos. Our children are often neglected. With carefully measured and intoned syllables, he articulately calls for a return to simple values—teamwork, sacrifice, love, putting others first, discipline, the Golden Rule. We are, he says, not beyond redemption. But first, each one of us must stop the game of blame.

"We must find the closet mirror," he says, "and stand in its reflection for a while. We've got to understand that each one of us is to blame. Until we do that we cannot move forward." A standing ovation follows the speech. Afterward, a line forms, fifty yards deep, and a shy and private man signs autographs. The flash of the Vivatars burns his eyes.

Mike Singletary came clean. He confessed to his wife and to his God. He was an impostor. His wife cried for a long time. Singletary knew that he hurt the people he loved the most. The pain was unlike any that he had ever known. And yet he knew, as forgiveness was extended and grief experienced, that God was doing a work in his life. He was becoming empty of himself. His pride was dissolving in the acid that is God's grace. The pain was immense; the acceptance incomparably sweet. The hole that remained, Singletary filled with God's wisdom. He wrote: "Now God was filling the void in me that had so long been filled by my ego, my sin, by the world. To this day I'm not entirely sure what happened, but I know I became a new man."

Humility was the wisdom to understand that he could not trust in himself. "I think the thing that I learned most is that God can be trusted. I've realized that every day is a new day, a blessing from God. We have to realize that, no matter who we are, we are weak. No matter how hard we try, we control nothing. Nothing. No matter how hard I try to secure my future, I could wake up the next day with a lump on my chest, be in the hospital and die. When we finally realize how weak we really are, then we realize how strong God is."

The breaking of Singletary's pride revolutionized his perspective. Life was still a matter of doing his very best, but the motivation had changed. What God gives to each one of us—gifts, possessions, power, money—is to be carefully used for His glory. Freed from the need to feed an overwhelming ego, he was freed up to obey and to serve others. For the first time in his life, he knew who he was in Jesus Christ. It meant that he could love, without strings. He says he began the process of becoming downwardly mobile for the sake of others and God's kingdom. "Downward mobility is the exchange of pride for servanthood," he says. "Humility has to be at the root of it."

Singletary's life is now centered on pleasing God. He understands that what has been given to him is not his own and he uses it the best he can for God's kingdom. He takes his responsibility seriously. He tithes consistently as a recognition that his money and possessions are not his own. He loves his wife and three children, for they clearly are his most cherished gifts. He donates to charities because he recognizes a Christian's responsibility to the hurting and poor. When he speaks at churches, he never charges money because he wants it known that the gospel is not for sale. He gives generously to individuals in need when prompted by the Holy Spirit. Into his comfortable home, he has taken his wife's grandparents and his niece, who had run into trouble. He stops to pick up a stranger whose car has broken down. None of this, however, is stated to make Singletary proud. He has had his fill of pride.

That does not mean that he never struggles. As one of the dominant players of the National Football League, he makes good money, has a nice home, nice cars, and nice clothes. How will the values of his children be affected? It is a constant struggle to find balance between excess and need. "As long as we don't horde what we have and are willing to give them up," he says, "then I don't feel like these things are a problem." But he still worries. And he constantly looks for other ways to use his resources—whether money, talents, or position—to have a greater influence for Christ. He is constantly aware of the stakes involved.

And, occasionally, he will still get a stab of pride. He has developed a technique to deal with it. "Every time someone praises me, I transfer that praise immediately to the Lord. I thank Him, for He is the one that has given me the ability to do what I do. That way the compliment never stops with me; it's just a continuous flow. I use it as an opportunity to remind myself where true strength comes from. It's not me. It's God."

There is the energy. Hundreds of teenagers, the undirected kind of chaos of lives caught in the tension. The pressure, the questions coming into focus, the internal brawling of child-adult. Mike Singletary is at church.

He knows that this is not just something to do to fill in the time. There will be no tackles he will make that will carry a greater force. Dressed in a color-striped shirt, a pair of jeans, he comes clothed in humility. He touches on reality: single parents, drugs, gangs, sex, violence. All the bombardments, the dangerous lives. He speaks, looking through no rose-colored glasses: "The consensus is that the young people are lost. That there is no hope." And then, almost beyond belief, he speaks of the choice of faith. The tough kind that doesn't compromise, that shatters all illusions of pride, that refuses to coddle, and, that finally stands.

"The thing that we have to do is get to the point of death," he says. "When we do, it is the same experience that Jesus Christ had. And then we will rise again."

It is, he humbly suggests, the only way to live.

OBEDIENCE

10

TO REALLY LIVE
IS TO BE READY TO DIE

"And became obedient to death—even death on a cross!"

—*Philippians 2:8*

Ours is a world of flux, of seas that churn and change, of seasons that slip one into another, of lives that move in steady motion from birth to death. A world, it seems, in continual transformation, where the only constant is change. And then we watch the evening news with its scattered monotones of violence, poverty, and disaster, and we see that there is one other constant: evil. Day after day, it ravages our planet. In a world of change, evil is the one thing we can count on.

Worse than evil's constancy is its depth. Author Philip Yancey tells the story of one man's coming to grip with its horror. Yancey interviewed a veteran of World War II, who was sent in to liberate and clean up

Dachau, the Nazi concentration camp where thousands of Jews were exterminated. This is what that man says:

"A buddy and I were assigned to a box car. Inside were human corpses stacked in neat rows, exactly like firewood. The Germans, ever meticulous, had planned out the rows, alternating the heads and the feet, accommodating the different sizes and shapes of bodies. Our job was like moving furniture. We would pick up each body—so light—and carry it to a designated area. Some fellows couldn't do this part. They stood by the barbed wire fences retching. I couldn't believe it the first time we came across a person in the pile still alive! But it was true. Incredibly, some of the corpses weren't corpses. They were human beings. We yelled for doctors and they went to work on these survivors right away. I spent two hours in that box car; two hours that for me included every known emotion: rage, pity, shame, revulsion. Every negative emotion, I should say. They came in waves . . . all but the rage . . . it stayed, fueling our work. We had no other emotional vocabulary for such a scene. After we had taken the few survivors to a makeshift clinic, we turned our attention to the Nazis: the SS officers in charge of Dachau. Our captain asked for a volunteer to escort a group of twelve SS officers to the interrogation center, and a guy named Chuck . . . his hand shot right up. Chuck claimed to have worked for Al Capone before the war and not one of us doubted it. Well, Chuck grabbed his machine gun and prodded the group of SS prisoners down the trail. They walked ahead of him with their hands locked behind their heads, their elbows sticking out on either side. A few minutes after they disappeared into the trees we heard the rattling burp of a machine gun and three long bursts of fire. Soon Chuck came strolling out, smoke still curling from the tip of his weapon. 'They all tried to run away,' he said with a kind of leer."

The scene convinced this soldier to go into the ministry. He continues, "It was on that day that I felt called by God to become a pastor. First there was the horror of the corpses in the boxcar: I could not absorb such a scene. I did not even know that such absolute evil existed! But when I saw it, I knew beyond a doubt, that I'd spend my life serving whatever opposed such evil . . . serving God. Then came the Chuck incident. I had a nauseating fear that the captain might call upon me to escort the next group of SS guards; and even a more dreadful fear that if he did, I might do the same thing that Chuck did! The beast that was in those guards was also in me. The beast within those guards, the beast within Chuck, the beast was also in me."

That soldier learned a lesson that most of us spend a lifetime avoiding: that the beast of evil slumbers in every one of us. Who, if we are painfully honest, can deny it? Maybe we aren't guilty of incinerating thousands of Jews, but how many times have we torn out a piece of someone's heart with a lie? How many times have we wished someone out of existence—a boss, a spouse, a mother-in-law—and allowed that wish to affect how we treated them? All of us, not that deep down inside, are driven by selfish desires, the spark and fuel of evil, the rage of Dachau.

In his book, *The Spirit of the Disciplines*, Dallas Willard makes a compelling argument that each of us is capable of great evil given the correct circumstances. He writes:

> Our "Why?" in the face of evil, then, signals a lack of insight—willing or unwilling—into the forces that inhabit the normal human personality and thereby move or condition the usual course of human events. Above all, it shows a failure to understand that the immediate support of the evils universally deplored lies in the simple *readiness* of "decent" individuals to harm others or allow harm to come to others when the conditions are "right." That readiness comes into play whenever it will help us realize our goals of security, ego gratification, or satisfaction of bodily desires. This systematic readiness that pervades the personality of normal, decent human beings is fallen human nature. [Dallas Willard, *The Spirit of the Disciplines: Understanding How God Changes Lives* (San Francisco: HarperCollins, 1989), p. 225]

God knows this. He says that the human heart is, above all else, desperately wicked. Even those of us who have acknowledged the darkness and turned to God for forgiveness are haunted by the shadows of evil. Our words speak of grace; our actions often sting and wound. We claim to be pure and humble servants, then complain when we get no applause. We pray for abundant life and chase after empty, self-indulgent dreams.

A HARD PARADOX

The disease of evil is rooted in our hearts. The Bible is insistent about that, and there is no easy cure.

Only Christ's blood, spilled from an innocent heart, is sufficient to overcome its power. But even Christ's death does not free us—in the here and now—from the effects of evil. Evil still has its world-tilting sway. And we still find ourselves vulnerable to its lure. Although repulsive, there is something about evil that fascinates us. We see movies with names like *Cape Fear* and *Fatal Attraction*. We tune into news of serial killings. We laugh, nervously, at cruel jokes and sick comedy. None of us can tune out evil's seductive whisper, its call to lead us into places we should not go and desires we cannot afford to fuel. The temptation of evil made no less a man than the apostle Paul cry out in frustration: "The good I wish to do, I don't always do. The evil I don't want to do, I wind up doing. These evil inclinations wage war against what I know God wants me to do. The war goes on inside me. Who will set me free?"

The question is a difficult one. The answer, even more so: Freedom comes through yielding our will to God and obeying a set of rules. Jesus stated it clearly: "If you love me, you will obey my commands." He did not mince words. Do you want to love Me? Then obey My commands. Do you want to be free from evil? Then do what I say.

Philippians, the book of paradoxes, says it yet again: The ticket to freedom is obedience. It's a hard one to swallow. You see, we thought we already knew all there was to know about freedom. We are, we tell ourselves, a liberated people. We honor rebels, buy radar detectors, smoke in the boys' rooms. We learned long ago that freedom comes from avoiding the rules, changing the rules, even breaking the rules, if we must. Obedience—following the rules—violates everything we stand for and it leads, we are convinced, to binding and restrictive slavery.

This thinking even creeps into our churches. Relationship is the en vogue word. Relationships, we tell ourselves, are the key to life—with God and with each other. And that is true. But in our haste to make our point, we sometimes neglect the concept of obedience. Notice what Jesus said: If you *love* Me, you will *obey* My commands. Although it is clear that obedience is to flow out of a loving relationship, there is in those words the distinct ring of authority. Jesus is not suggesting obedience; He is demanding it.

He does the same thing in the Sermon on the Mount. *Love your enemies*, He says. *Reconcile broken relationships. Stand firm against the lure of money, power, or fame. Seek the kingdom of God above all else. When you are wronged, don't seek revenge.* Try reading the sermon as if you are reading it for the first time. Really think about what Jesus is asking. The commands seem shocking, the demands nearly impossible to meet.

LOVE'S RULES

Jesus' demanding tone seems harsh. But that's just because He sees the truth more clearly than we do. The beast of evil is within each of us. The blood of Jesus can wash us clean, but it cannot easily keep us from our dirty work. The appeal of sin, of sidestepping God and fulfilling our own selfish desires, is much too strong to be taken lightly. It is only through obedience, as Jesus knows, that we can tame the beast within us.

God's rules are not meant to be restrictive, but protective. We are enormously prone to hurting ourselves and those around us. We can self-destruct at the drop of a dime, or at least a dollar or two. God's rules, His commandments, flow out of His love for us. They are not just for His sake, but for ours as well. He wants to protect us from unnecessary heartache, destruction, and violence. I believe that all of God's rules are designed either to protect us from harming ourselves, to keep us from hurting others, or to rescue us from wasting our lives.

Think about some of the rules designed to keep us from harming ourselves: Don't let anger and bitterness take root, do not go deeply into debt, stay free of addictions. When we break these rules, we risk pain and brokenness. Self-worth deteriorates and we suffer from remorse, self-pity, and depression.

Rules keeping us from hurting others help to build community and unite Christians in love. The Bible commands us, for example, to speak the truth to one another in love, to put the interests of others before our own, to be generous to the poor. If we ignore these rules, we find ourselves set adrift, cut off from the stability and strength and support we gain when we live peacefully and work joyfully with others.

Finally, there are the laws that keep us from squandering what God has given us. Be the salt of the earth, Jesus tells us. Be lights to the world. Stay clear of the applause of men. Do good deeds constantly. Let people know that I live in you. In a phrase, God calls us to be difference makers in our world. He tells us, for example, to turn the world's order of greed, selfishness, and hate on its head, and to make people, not things, our priority. For me, these are some of the most powerful commands in the Bible. I have periodically awakened in the middle of the night, drenched in a cold sweat, at the horror of wasting the life God has given me in a series of trivial pursuits. I have only one chance to live, and I want to make it count. I thank God for His commands that show me how to make a difference in our broken world.

RISKY FAITH

It is clear, then, that God's commands flow from His love for us. They protect us from ourselves and our uncommonly human tendencies to damage and trivialize. But I believe there is more to obedience than just defensive strategies. I don't think that protecting us from evil was God's only reason for demanding that we follow His rules. Hebrews 5:8 states, "Although he [Jesus] was a son, he learned obedience from what he suffered." For the longest time I have puzzled over that verse. Clearly Christ's obedience was not to tame a beast of evil within Him. This is an obedience of a much higher sort, designed not to protect, not to defend us from evil, but rather to activate us, to put us on the offense—to transform us into active warriors against evil.

This obedience is far harder than the defensive kind because it is far more risky. In a world twisted with evil, selfishness, and ignorance, acts of love and wisdom—acts in line with God's will—seem, at best, out of place, and require tremendous energy, imagination, and faith. More faith than most of us think we have. To paraphrase Hebrews 11:1: "Faith is believing in the unseen." That's what God calls us to do. In a concrete world of paychecks and power brokers and bleeding ulcers, He calls us to live our lives with a conviction of invisible hope. He calls us to fight evil, to do good, to buck systems, trusting that in the end it will make a difference.

God knows the risk of faith. In a human frame of capillaries and neurons, susceptible to pain and grief and fatigue, Jesus learned that this world does not make friends with acts of faith. He obeyed out of faith, in the face of seen realities that broke His heart and ripped away at His body: persecution, hatred, violence, and finally, death. Faith, His unseen compass, often led Him into places that He would just as soon not have been: Gethsemane, Lazarus' tomb, the cross. Jesus suffered for following the path of faith, immeasurably so. He tasted His own blood, wept at death, and reeled with pain. He learned, to a degree that few of us learn it, exactly what faith requires: everything, and then some. But His suffering taught Him obedience.

WHERE DID GOD GO?

Suffering, faith, and obedience were intermingled and woven daily into the fabric of Jesus' life. But what about our lives? When obedience involves suffering, do we have the faith to trust God for the outcome? When faith calls us out on the limb of suffering, are we willing to respond with obedience? We who, at our best, might be willing to trade *Monday Night Football* for a Bible study. We who, at our worst, would exchange our faith for a bigger home or a miracle cure. We live not only with our own sin, but in a world of trouble. There are times—and it is most of the time—when the possibility of faith is strangled in the day-to-day grind of it all. Our marriages often rock back and forth between routine and fury, and we wonder where the spark will come from to restore the passion. Many of us live with afflictions, both real and imagined, that cause us to reel in pain, indignation, and embarrassment. Some of us go to work each day, bored to our socks or stressed out of our heads, and wonder secretly if insanity is a justified cause for disability. Some of our children have become obsessed with music that rocks our house with restlessness and anger. Some of us are alone, the silence so thick it threatens to suffocate us. Some of us are facing bankruptcies, depressions, separations and bereavements. And worse yet, we can look around and see those without faith prospering and happy.

Faith, if we are honest, sometimes seems like a candle in the rain, hissing for air. The more we try to see by this invisible light, the more we seem to stumble. Faith, we begin to feel, might work on another planet, one that contains less chaos and fewer broken dreams. It's not so much that we doubt God's power—we still get an occasional glance or two at a cloudless night sky. It's more a matter of how it works itself out in our lives, in our twenty-four-hour scrapes with reality. We want to believe, really believe, that God wants the best in our lives—His will. But right in the middle of our prayers for power to do it, the baby cries, the thunder claps, the fury breaks. Our good intentions are overwhelmed by complications.

The truth is, Christians can try to apply everything we have discussed in this book, and still be burdened with pain, fear, and desperation. There comes a point where faith just seems to make no sense. We have tried and tried, and yet nothing seems to work out right. We begin to question the reality of God in our lives.

POWER ALONG THE WAY

God knows. The Bible is filled with the stories of humans such as us—desperate, hurting, prone to sin, thirsting after God, broken, and wanting to be healed. In embarrassing detail, the Bible offers the human-ness—the frailty, the sinfulness, and the tragedy. Jacob is a conniver. Moses feels inadequate. Peter acts like a headstrong fool. David has blood on his hands. But it is in this context of human weakness and sin that the Bible dares to make the radical assertion that faith—the kind that reshapes hearts and the direction of history—*is* possible. Even after many, many failures and disap-pointments. Jacob becomes a pivot point for God's plan. Moses pulls off one of the greatest escapes in his-tory. The church is built on Peter's leadership. David is called a man "after God's heart."

Those stories often make us feel even more guilty, more hopeless. We, too, pray for transformation and, instead, are overwhelmed in frustration. We can't seem to rise above our day-to-day lives to grasp the re-ality of faith. I don't believe it's a question of sincerity: we really *want* God to transform us. It is, rather, a ques-tion of process. Most of us pray and pray, and then wait. For what, we're not sure—a mystical sense of en-ergy, perhaps, or a revolutionary thought, or a surge of power from God—but we wait . . . and wait. And more times than not, we remain trapped and exhausted at square one.

The problem is the waiting, the standing still. Transforming faith, the Bible tells us, happens only in the context of movement. The power of God comes to those who obey. And obedience means taking action— to love one another, to restore a relationship, to confront a person in sin. God promises to give us power as we act. That, of course, is not our preference: We would rather that God provide power *before* we move. God, however, has always required a movement of faith.

Joshua 3 provides a classic illustration. The children of Israel, after decades of wandering in the wilderness, had finally received clearance to move into the promised land. God instructs Joshua to march toward the border of Canaan and occupy the land. There is only one problem. The border of Canaan just happens to be marked by the Jordan River, which just happens to be at flood stage. And there is no bridge, no boat, no ferry, no scuba equipment. The command from God comes to Joshua to organize the people in a straight line behind the Ark of the covenant and march directly toward the raging waters in a beeline to Canaan. The promise is this: Somewhere along the way, God will intervene. But Israel must first take steps of faith. In fact, it was only when the people in the front of the line had actually entered the river that God miraculously parted the waters.

There are many other examples. Moses and the Red Sea. Jesus healing the lepers only after they traveled to the priests in obedience to His command. The men who lowered down their sick friend through the roof. Jesus praying at Gethsemane. The power of God came only as people *acted* on their faith. Power along the way.

God wants to supernaturally intervene in the difficulties and challenges of our everyday lives—but He can't until we first demonstrate faith by walking forward on the path of obedience. Out of our paralysis of pain or fear or disillusionment, we must take the first step of faith. A relationship cannot be reconciled unless we first pick up the phone, no matter how timid or inadequate or terrified of confrontation we feel. Sexual sin does not disappear unless we make a conscious move to stop before we go too far. Addictions cannot be overcome unless we first make a step to get the right kind of help. We must act on the promise that God can do all things through Christ who strengthens us. It sounds impossible. Scary. Some of us would rather walk into a raging river than do what we need to do. But God promises power along the way.

Raw obedience is necessary because we are creatures who tend to prefer the status quo, no matter how miserable it is. There is a part of each of us that prefers being buried alive than being out on a dead limb. Even in fear, pain, and isolation, there is the certainty of the known. Faith is, by its very definition, risky: We are asked, by setting our invisible sight, to move into God's promises. We are asked to do His will, with nothing to rely on but His Word, and without knowing whether His plan will lead us to healing or to a tomb. That is the rub. We don't know where His plan will lead us. And we can't know, until we get there. But we can know this: He will provide the power along the way. And He will lead us into joy.

Profile:
Lorrie Shaver

LORRIE SHAVER: DELTA FLIGHT 191

"I've realized . . . just how finite we really are and how much we have to commit our lives daily to Him. It's not a tomorrow thing. I need to realize today I need to live for Him and what really matters to God is if I am obedient in today's call."

—*Lorrie Shaver*
in a tape-recorded message sent shortly
before her death, to a missionary in France

*T*he phone rang in Patty Bender's house about 10 P.M., August 2, 1985. It startled her out of a nap. She fought the slow haze that follows half-sleep. The television pulsating impossible shadows; the movie she couldn't remember; the kids were in bed.

She heard her husband, Phil, answer the phone: "Oh, hi!" She knew, by the tone of his voice, it was her mom. Probably just wanted to chat. Phil wasn't talking a lot, just uh-huhs and yeahs. "Let me have the phone," Patty said. Her husband said no.

"Okay," he said into the phone, "we'll talk to you tomorrow." He hung up.

"What's wrong?" Patty asked. "Lorrie's been in a plane accident" was the answer. "We don't know if she's a survivor or not."

Lorrie. The girl who was always up to old tricks. Patty remembered the time in high school when she told Lorrie she was going out on a date and the places they were going. Lorrie got the gang together. At the movie, at the restaurant, on the road, Patty and her date were being followed. Lorrie never made a sound. Patty could feel the laughter. That was Lorrie, always having a good time.

After the phone call, Patty Bender was hysterical. They watched the news—an L-1011, Delta Flight 191, had crashed in Dallas. The pictures were horrible. The only survivors, the anchor man dead-panned, were in the smoking section. Patty got mad, real mad. She had lost a lifetime friend. Her husband tried to comfort her; he prayed.

"I kept screaming 'why?' Why could God let this happen to Lorrie? She was getting ready to go to France and serve Him as a missionary. Why? How could God do this?"

It wasn't that Patty didn't believe the answer— heaven. The answer wasn't the problem, the question was.

Lorrie's old tricks. Patty can remember countless walks on the Florida beach near their childhood homes. They listened to the waves. They giggled a lot. The stars, sometimes, made them talk of God. And they shared problems; Patty can't even remember them . . . they seem so insignificant now. What she does remember, more than anything else, was that Lorrie was always there.

Always loving.

After the news of the crash, Patty fell asleep in an uneasy mixture of anger and love. She dreamed of a plane accident.

"I remember a horrible explosion and I kept seeing fire."

"The eye is the lamp of the body. If your eyes are good, your whole body will be full of light."
—*Matthew 6:22*

Lorrie Shaver was not spectacular in appearance. She was overweight and wore, for the most part, pullover shirts, corduroy jeans, and work boots. Her hands were sliced and stained and calloused, fingernails short and stubby—the hands of a girl who worked with boxes at a Florida grocery store. Her eyes were small, and she had freckles.

The same is true of her actions: nothing spectacular. She never saved anyone from drowning; she worked hard for grades at college; she wasn't creative, she had few original ideas.

"She was as average a girl as they come," says her pastor, Paul Mutchler. "She was totally vanilla. There were no special gifts or talents—except for one. And that was love. She loved people specifically, and that made her very special."

She loved, her friends say, not because it was a special gift. She loved because she worked hard at it. She was obedient. Seldom did her love ask for a spotlight.

"Lorrie was a person that entered into your life by the back door," one friend says. "She didn't come on real strong, but she made her presence known. She wasn't imposing; she didn't require your time; she was just there and became your friend."

That commitment showed itself daily in "little" things." She had an instinct for knowing when people were hurting.

The time when one of her friends was new in Florida and her parents, who lived in another state, had just divorced. It was Christmas, and Lorrie came to visit. On a drive to the beach, Lorrie said little, but she listened a lot.

The first anniversary of the death of a friend's father, Lorrie would write a note. The second anniversary, a phone call.

Lorrie seemed to have a gift for making the commonplace uncommon: making well-timed phone calls; spotting strangers in church; giving friends rides in her jeep; listening to an endless procession of problems . . . day after day. Over and over.

"She had the uncanny ability to make people feel special," says one friend.

Lorrie loved with a laugh. She enjoyed life.

"You could usually tell when she arrived somewhere even if you couldn't see her," says a former youth pastor of Lorrie's. "There was usually a ruckus in the area around her because she was always clowning around with everyone."

She laughed a great deal. When she threw a friend in the ocean. When they couldn't get the VCR to work. When she went to the store and her friends acted like they were from New Zealand. Putting the top down on her jeep when it was thirty degrees.

"I may forget a lot of things about Lorrie," says one friend. "But I'll never forget her laugh."

"I can still picture Lorrie coming into the office and, cocking her head back, saying 'Hi, pastor.' She had that look that I never knew if she was coming in with a prayer request or a bucket of water."

That was Lorrie.

The soft touch of calloused hands. The bright sparkle of small eyes.

Old tricks.

"No sorrow will ever disturb me, no trial ever disarm me, no circumstance will ever cause me to fret, for I shall rest in the joy of my Lord."
—*from a plaque on Lorrie Shaver's bedroom wall*

Lorrie Shaver told her pastor she loved her parents even more because she was adopted. She was premature at birth, weighing three pounds. Her father, Fred, remembers his first trip to the hospital to see Lorrie. "I noticed a real little tiny thing over in the corner and I pointed it out to my wife. Well, it turned out that it was a syringe with a blanket over it." And then he saw Lorrie, and fell in love. "She was beautiful."

The love grew. Fred can't recall any special times, just a steady, unquestioning, always growing love.

"Her mom and her had a special relationship," Fred says. Lorrie and her mom shared devotions together, and dreams. And, more than anything, love. Lorrie's silly little drawings in school were Picassos to her mom. Her mom was proud of Lorrie, especially in college. She would call often and tell her so and encourage her in her schoolwork.

The love grew.

During her sophomore year in college, Lorrie's mom died. Lorrie retreated to the beach, where she went to weep for her mother. Alone, as the waves whispered eternal rhythms, she broke down. The hurt of missing her mom never completely vanished. She longed for a reunion.

More than anything, Lorrie Shaver wanted to do some small thing for the Lord. Kent and Becky Good, who grew up in her home church, were missionaries to France. She began to seek them out. "During missions conference I stayed in Lorrie's dorm room," says Becky Good. "She began asking me some serious questions about France. Could she be used as a missionary?" Becky remembers one conversation lasting until two in the morning. Later, Lorrie went to France to attend the Euro-Missions Conference. While attending the conference, she saw the tremendous spiritual need in the country. By the time the conference had ended she had made a decision: She wanted to be a missionary in France.

Despite their love for Lorrie, Kent and Becky had reservations. They thought she would have problems with the language. Becky filled out a recommendation for Lorrie for the foreign missions board. She stated their reservation. The Goods, however, were aware of Lorrie's strong point: her ability to love. While she was in France she had communicated that love without the language.

"She left behind more people that knew her and still ask about her than any of the others who have come through," Kent says. "There is a shopkeeper in Chalon who still asks about her: 'And how's—I can't remember her name. You know, the girl with the laughing eyes.'"

A few days after filling out the recommendation, Becky Good called the foreign missions board.

The girl with the laughing eyes would probably make a wonderful missionary. That was the gist of what she said. A short time later, she was appointed a missionary to France.

Lorrie Shaver was looking forward to the future. She was excited about France, almost obsessed. Her friends remember her passion.

They had to stop and buy croissants. And look at an endless number of French posters. "And then," she would say, "this is what they do in France." She wrote to missionaries and friends in France often.

"She made me realize that to be a missionary, the people have to consume your thoughts. They must pull you," says a friend.

But, if Lorrie Shaver gave a conscious message in the last few months of her life, it was not one centered on the future.

That message, by words and actions, was simply: Today, live for the Lord. Each minute, each action, must be surrendered to the Lord.

On deputation, when Lorrie talked about her plans to the people in the churches, she played a recording of a song, "Tomorrow." A line in the lyrics goes:

I'll give my life tomorrow.
What about today?

Lorrie Shaver hated good-byes. They made her nervous, jumpy for the right words.

Leaving for France would be difficult.

"I am excited about leaving for France," Lorrie said in a tape to a missionary in Europe, "but at the same time, it's hard to bring those things up to friends and family members. Breaking ties with people [is hard]—even though you know that if they are of the Lord it's not a final thing."

Saying good-bye to family would be the toughest. But Lorrie found consolation in one fact: Her brother and sister-in-law were supposed to have their baby before Lorrie was to leave for France.

She already had a card picked out for the new dad and mom. On the outside was a picture of a beaver. Goofy, bucktoothed smile. Inside was the caption, "Congratulations on the little shaver."

It was the first time Lorrie was to be an aunt. She told a friend that she couldn't wait to touch a little hand.

A few weeks before she was to leave for France, Lorrie was to be commissioned as a missionary at a conference in Colorado. She booked a plane for Denver with a layover in Dallas.

She was to leave about a week before conference was to start. It would give her time to visit a high school friend, who was struggling some spiritually. And she could also surprise Kent and Becky Good, who were scheduled to speak in Denver about missionary work in France.

That was Lorrie.

Old tricks.

A few days before she left for the conference, Lorrie Shaver was at the beach with a friend. That was nothing new. She loved the beach. Lorrie told her friend that, in all of her life, she never felt as much in God's will as she did then. As the waves found the shore, Lorrie said she was certain she was doing exactly what God wanted her to do.

She said she was at peace.

"He causes his sun to rise on the evil and the good, and sends rain on the righteous and the unrighteous."

—*Matthew 5:45*

After the plane crash, Fred Shaver had been to Dallas. He had flown in over the crashed plane. He had met with the airline, and he got the final devastating report. The lady in Dallas had gone to check the list of survivors. Fred had waited a few minutes, and she came back shaking her head. Lorrie wasn't on the list. He took some comfort in the fact that they had found some money on Lorrie's body. That meant she wasn't completely burned.

Now he was driving back from the Fort Lauderdale airport. The same airport where he had last seen his daughter a few days earlier. He remembered they had hugged and the glasses that he had in his pocket jabbed Lorrie.

They laughed.

And Lorrie told him that she loved him. She always did that, Fred says, and she always meant it. She walked away with that same grin. And, looking over her shoulder, said, "Bye, Dad. I'll see you later."

It was evening now—the sky a soft flame, and Fred was driving Sunset Strip. He was thinking about Lorrie—the way she laughed, the people that she cared about, the little baby who seldom cried, the practical jokes.

Fred remembered looking out his car window. Scattered along the sidewalks, random stumbling, were bums.

"Rejoice with those who rejoice; mourn with those who mourn."

—Romans 12:15

"Jesus wept."

—John 11:35

After the memorial service, Patty Bender went to the Shavers' house. The service was standing room only; now it was only a handful of Lorrie's closest friends. They reminisced until nearly midnight. They laughed and laughed. During the evening, Patty, for the first time, was joyful. "It was there that it hit me—

Lorrie's in heaven," Patty says. "And heaven meant something to me then."

Patty still couldn't explain the whys. Obedience, sometimes, just didn't make sense. She knew that her friend's death had changed her: "She taught me what was really important in life." And as the sound of laughter filtered through a Florida summer night, so did Patty's anger.

Old tricks.

"The grass withers and the flowers fall, because the breath of the LORD blows on them. Surely the people are grass. The grass withers and the flowers fall, but the word of our God stands forever."
—Isaiah 40:7-8

Fred Shaver is a solid man, quiet, white-haired, a chuckler. He works for an electric company. He is a man familiar with grief. Before Lorrie's death, he and his wife lost an infant child, which was followed by miscarriages.

And then baby Lorrie. Adopted into a family that loved her with all they had. They had many years of memories. And then Fred's wife died. Time had made the hurt bearable.

And then the plane crash. Lorrie, the lady in Dallas said, was not on the list.

He has no answers why. He doesn't even pretend. Fred doesn't have a theological mind, only a simple and trusting faith, and the hope that some good will come out of Lorrie's death. He has heard about personal commitments and revival. He hopes it's true.

The grief, Fred says, has taught him one thing above all else: "All you can do is depend on your reward in heaven—we'll be back together again in the presence of the Lord. It's got to be beautiful. I don't know how you live without that thought. There is nothing around this world that has any permanence to it. Nothing."

"'For my thoughts are not your thoughts, neither are your ways my ways,' declares the LORD. 'As the heavens are higher than the earth, so are my ways higher than your ways and my thoughts than your thoughts.'"

—*Isaiah 55:8–9*

After the graveside services, the Shaver family walked the short distance to the grave of Lorrie's mom. Fred, Jr., and Brenda, noticeably pregnant. And Johnny, Lorrie's younger brother, who had to deal with the death of his mother and sister, all before the age of eighteen.

And Fred.

Lorrie's with you now. Rejoicing in the presence of the Lord. That's what they said.

And then they wept.

"A woman giving birth to a child has pain because her time has come; but when her baby is born she forgets the anguish because of her joy that a child is born into the world. So with you: Now is your time of grief, but I will see you again

*and you will rejoice, and no one will take away
your joy."*

—John 16:21–22

A couple of weeks after Lorrie Shaver's death, her nephew was born. Fred Shaver marveled at the beauty of the newborn.

JOY

12

REWARD
OR GIFT?

"Therefore God exalted him to the highest place."
—Philippians 2:9

*T*racy Blackburn, at a relatively early age, thought she had a firm grip on joy. She had, at the very least, the trappings of success. She drove a BMW, wore the most stylish clothes, and lived the lifestyle of the jet-setter she had become. This life was beyond her wildest dream, and she was, as dreamers go, a pretty wild one. As a high-ranking executive with a leading investment company, she had the world at her fingertips. "I couldn't fathom life without all those wonderful, glorious perks," she says. She had power and respect, the precise addictions she felt she needed. The formula for joy.

Or so she thought. That was before her blood pressure and weight soared; her power and health slipped away. The American Dream, she began to learn, was exceedingly costly. The pace, pressure, and competition began to outrank the glorious perks. Her status as A Very Important One, in a nearly literal sense, was shot to pieces. Her doctor told her to change her lifestyle. Immediately. She always had respect for deadlines, especially the kind that race across a heart monitor. The day she quit her job, she prayed to a God she was not sure was there. It was a plea for help. How could she now find joy? She had watched the American dream disintegrate in a mixture of exhaustion and pain. If she could no longer count on her bankbook for personal worth, what then? It is a question that echoes across our country with a ring of desperation.

The American Dream, once precise and achievable, has increasingly become the American Mirage. In the fifties, nearly everyone agreed that a three-bedroom suburban home with a white picket fence, a golden retriever, and a Ford station wagon made the Dream come true. Dad went to work from eight to four, and Mom stayed home to care for the children and bake chocolate chip cookies. Weekends were for church, scouts, and family camping trips. The American Dream was, with any luck or brains at all, rather uncomplicated and certainly achievable.

No longer. At the end of the eighties, that decade marked by unbridled American Dreamers, *Time* magazine ran a compelling story about what had become of the American Dream. Although still very much intact, the magazine stated, the Dream had become almost prohibitively expensive. While housing, medical, and tuition costs had skyrocketed, inflation had chewed a hole in the average American's pocketbook. No longer could the Dream be achieved by one working parent. Forty-hour work weeks were unthinkable. Debt was almost always necessary.

But still, the American Dream retained its appeal. Television, with its penchant for images, embedded its message in our nearly unconscious brains. Things satisfy, the tube told us, and more things satisfy even more. If there was any doubt, we had only to look at the smiling people in the ads—self-satisfied, slightly smug, and about to burst with joy. All from owning things. The right things. Flashy and brilliant things. Technological things. Things that catch the unique you. In the eighties, the meaning of "necessity" had changed. VCRs, microwaves, entertainment centers, CD players, and big screen televisions were no longer considered luxuries. The American Dreamer *needed* them. Add in the cost of a couple of reasonably decent cars (at least $20,000 each), a health club membership, Disneyland vacations, college expenses, a swimming pool, and you can quickly see that the American Dream carried a far higher price tag than it had before.

Achieving it no longer required a halfhearted effort, but a heartless one. The Dreamer had to make a nearly kamikaze-like commitment to acquiring the dollars needed to buy it. All other commitments—to God, family, or leisure—had to be sacrificed to the Idol of Things. There were no shortcuts or accidental successes. The American Dream consumed the consumers, and turned them into mechanical and broken puppets. Almost literally.

SUCCESS STORIES

Recently I received a letter from a forty-three-year-old man with a $300,000 annual income. He said that in the last fifteen years he had owned more than a dozen Corvettes, boats, airplanes, and homes across the country. But unlike the smiling actors in the ads, he was not able to find joy. Another letter came from a twenty-four-year-old woman with an annual salary of $80,000. She had bought a new car, a new house, and, she thought, all the joy her money could buy. But there was one thing she hadn't counted on: the regret and guilt of living a self-centered life.

There is a sense of tragic irony here. Dream chasers relentlessly seek comfort, pleasure, power, and security. And most end up feeling inexplicably alienated, filled with regret and pain, powerless and insecure. Each year, I talk with hundreds of people who have chased the American Dream. More often than not, they are broken people shattered by the hidden costs of "success." One man recently had to choke back tears while he talked to me. All his life he had tried to make it to "Easy Street." Every waking moment of his days was spent trying to achieve his dream. It's not that he didn't love his wife and children; on the contrary, he wanted to provide what was best for them. They could wait awhile until he achieved all those wonderful things they deserved. He should have been happy as he spoke with me. He was just a deal away from the big time, a breath away from a vice presidency, one client away from Easy Street. And he had just taken possession of his dream home. The only problem was that it was an empty home. His wife and children had left him, and he was alone with the echoes of his footsteps.

The price tag of his dream had cost him everything of value. He found himself spiritually alienated, relationally isolated, emotionally drained, and physically broken. All that was left was a pile of things that mocked him.

Many of the stories of the "successful" end that way. But what about those who weren't so "fortunate," those who, for reasons of ability, temperament, economic class, or discrimination, were blocked from pursuing the Dream. In our society, we can find them just about anywhere. In their easy chairs, stuffing themselves with electronic images of success and Doritos, a junk diet of stars and famous homes and everything they are not. Or in the back streets, slashing their way from obscurity with a knife or a gun. Or on the sidelines, watching the graceful moves of athletes from the top of a beer. Even those disqualified from obtaining the Dream are diseased by it. The symptoms run from numbness, to anger, to resignation, to an inexplicable need to tease themselves mad by focusing on whatever it is they can't have.

Despite evidence of ruin, the American Dream still lingers, because it feeds into our inbred desire to move up, to take care of Number One, to secure our own happiness—no matter what price we have to pay. Why do we continue to do it? The Bible answers bluntly: We are sinners. We were born with hearts that drift naturally toward self-protection and self-promotion. Personal comfort and security seem so important to us that we will do nearly anything to acquire them. When it comes to push and shove, we're more than willing to push and shove.

In slightly milder terms, it's called selfishness. And sadly, it's a disease that affects more than just individuals. As we emerge from the eighties—a decade of unabashed Dream chasing—we can see clearly the damage to our society. Self-indulgence has led to collective misery. The poor are poorer. Ethics have slipped. Productivity has dropped. Divorces are up and children suffer separation and pain. These problems cannot be blamed exclusively on the American Dream, of course. But it is obvious that a climate that encourages self-indulgence will, in the end, self-destruct. Jesus said that.

SURPRISED BY JOY

Fortunately, as individuals and as a society, we are waking up to the nightmare of the American Dream, to the bankruptcy of the more is better equation, and to the futility of sacrificing our lives at the Altar of Things. As we approach the twenty-first century, many people are looking for options. Volunteerism is increasing. Simpler lifestyles are in style. Spirituality is not just something to laugh at. The consensus seems to be this: There must be more to life than unabated consumerism. Joy is, quite possibly, something that refuses to be bought.

These trends have the potential for both good and bad. The good is obvious: Individuals and society benefit whenever relationships take priority over things. But danger often comes in a soft disguise. The new arrangement of priorities will succeed only if it follows a change of heart. It is, essentially, a question of motivation. Although the mood of the country may be changing, the desire of individuals remains the same: to find joy. And that is fine. God wants us to find joy, too. But if we serve others just so we can be joyful, isn't this just another, slightly more subtle form of selfishness? And how long will we continue to serve if it causes discomfort, inconvenience, and pain? What will happen if the person we are serving does not express gratitude? Will we lose our joy—and thus our motivation for serving?

The difficulty in discussing joy is that while we know that God offers joy as a reward for pure and selfless service, we also learn that if we serve for the sake of the reward, we'll miss it. The paradox of joy is that you can't find it by looking for it. It is not something that can be manipulated or depends on the correct arrangement of circumstances. Joy requires more than an agenda, even if the agenda is serving others.

Joy—the deep, sustaining joy that Jesus promised—is a gift from God that takes us by surprise. When is it most likely to surprise us? When we are striving, with all our heart and with each passing breath, to live like Jesus did: to lay down our lives freely for others, to live selflessly, without thought for our rewards. Sound difficult? The Bible says that without the proper motivation it is not only difficult, but impossible. The motivation must change from "my will be done" to "God's will be done." It must flow from a heart willing to descend, a heart that wants, more than anything else, to glorify God through how it loves.

In Philippians 2:6–8, the descent of Jesus—from heaven to hell, from God to man, from Creator to corpse—is vividly documented. It is not until verse 9

181

that exaltation, that most intense form of joy, is promised: "Therefore God exalted him to the highest place." The key word here is the transition, "therefore." It was only after a pure descent—motivated by selfless love and a desire to honor God—that the greatness of joy was fully realized.

OFFENSIVE JOY

To take our understanding of joy one step further, we need to begin with a redefinition. Too often, we have defined joy in the negative: an absence of pain, hunger, discomfort, and monotony. When we define joy in such a way, we spend most of our time building defenses: earning money to pay the bills, acquiring prestige so someone will remember our names, making a joke when someone gets too close. Avoiding *dis*ease becomes our number one priority: Deep relationships might bring hurt, risks might lead to disasters, confrontations aren't worth the trouble, faith and other things unseen lead to delusions. We get numbed, sidetracked, entertained, lost in the masses, enthralled, obsessed . . . anything to keep from facing anything that hurts.

But if we view joy as the avoidance of pain, we face a major problem. Avoidance requires barriers. And barriers, no matter how well constructed, tend to keep out the good stuff as well as the bad. Let's say we get burned in a relationship, and the pain drives us to vow never to get close to anyone again. Up goes the barrier. We're safe. No more pain. But also no more companionship, no more laughter, no more shared secrets—no more love. All the barrier leaves us is an aching emptiness.

The Bible doesn't play it so safe. When it comes to defining joy, there is a certain wildness, a near recklessness in its choice of words. Joy is framed in the positive: be, do, trust, risk, love. From the biblical perspective, joy is not *de*fensive, but rather inherently *of*fensive. Barriers are to be broken down, not erected. Instead of hiding in safe corners, we run toward life at full speed, embracing whatever it offers. Life in its fullness demands fullness of experience. It demands that we actively involve ourselves in God's will, and God's will is—if nothing else—wildly experiential.

The problem with defining joy in the positive is that because we live in a sinful world, experiencing the fullness of life means experiencing pain and failure. But Jesus knew that—and still He talked about joy. What we need to remember is that the joy He talked about was different. It had little to do with satisfying short-term desires and impulses, and everything to do with pleasing God. Jesus came to do only one thing—what His Father wanted Him to do. With an unshakable determination to do God's will, He chose the thorny and lonely path that demanded everything. While others were in the bushes confusing joy with pleasure, Jesus walked the hard road with commitment, purpose, discipline, and consistency. He knew that in the end, beyond the cross, was a joy that could rock even the deepest grave. One can only imagine, deep into an evening with His friends, the quality of Jesus' laughter. It was at least equal to the salt of His tears.

DREAMING BIG

Jesus did not try to manufacture joy, as if it required only raw materials. He understood that regardless of what He did, joy would not come on command. Jesus' commitment to do God's will was, at its core, a move of abandonment. He abandoned Himself to God's care, believing that He would provide for His needs—regardless of circumstance, depth of emotion, or violation. More than any other man in history, He risked trust. He believed that God would provide, against all odds, even against sin's vicious beast of death. Jesus trusted. And joy came as a gift.

Paradoxically, Jesus' dependence on God freed Him. It streamlined Him to serve. Released through faith from the demands of appetite and security, He was free to dream not the small and petty stuff of the Dream chasers, but the revolutionary dream of loving like God: freeing the enslaved, healing the diseased, giving sight to those stumbling in confusion, feeding the hungry, raising the dead, giving hope to those in shadows, mending hearts. By losing His life—truly losing it for the sake of others—He found it in all its fullness. And stumbled upon an unshakable joy.

How big is your dream? Is it the puny, selfish, doomed one named the American Dream? Is it the ceaseless, numbing pursuit of pleasure? Or are you so drained of energy and courage that you don't dream at all anymore? The Bible is a book about wild dreams, filled with the extraordinary dreams of God: to send His Son to earth, to become friends with humans, to love without condition, to transform hearts, to destroy sin. All so that you and I can risk a bigger, better dream. A dream that will surprise us with joy.

Profile:
John and Gwenn Tindall

13

JOHN AND GWENN TINDALL: RECEIVING JOY IN BROKENNESS

"Isn't joy more meaningful against a backdrop of pain? If you lived life on a permanent high, when would you know the thrill of joy?"

—Gwenn Tindall

*I*t was at the pre-grand opening of The Body Electric that Gwenn Schumacher got a case of the nerves. The serious kind—the heebie-jeebies, the willy-nillies, the kind that rattle around the stomach like a swallowed wasp. The massage, as if it needed to be stated, didn't work: $17.50—with the half-off coupon—and one hour of her wedding day down the drain.

Now, in the parking lot, in the grayness of an asphalt sky, her muscles slam-dancing the red alert, she has once again retreated to prayer. She presses her head to the steering wheel. At times such as these, her resiliency (nearly legendary by necessity) takes the form of rapid-fire pleading and praise. *Thanks, Father, for my kids. . . . Help them to feel safe and loved. . . . Thanks for John, help the wedding to go well. . . . Thanks for the many miracles you have performed in my life. . . . You know I am feeling overwhelmed right now, give me peace. . . . And, Father, please help me to get my hair right. . . . Amen.*

It's more of a conversation, really, than a prayer. No thees or thous, just deeply felt needs, no matter how small, and a personal history connecting prayer with nothing less than survival.

She turns the ignition and the conversation. The wedding night. "As long as the lights are low," she says, "I should be okay." She laughs a laugh of nervous anticipation, brimming with the clumsy up-and-down tones of anxiety and joy.

John Tindall is, for the most part, a logical kind of guy. Cool, reasoned, given to turtlenecks and bill-paying, the kind of guy you could feel comfortable with, say, at an amusement park. Or a foxhole. He composes his thoughts, eats ice cream with a certain methodical panache. This day of his wedding to Gwenn Schumacher—November 16—is, in many ways, just another day. He sits in the kitchen, sipping apple juice and wrapping in silver the gift from Frederick's: very un-Hollywood, no sweating palms or smirks, just a smile that feels, upon dissipation, like silk.

For a man who has tumbled from the heights, things seem settled.

On the surface, John and Gwenn, hours before their wedding, seem to share little more than an appointment for a never-ending bond. On nearly every outward level, there is diversity. Gwenn is thirty-eight, widowed with two children; John is twenty-seven. Gwenn is precise and well-ordered, concerned about minutiae, harboring some uncertainty about what others may think. John is looser, almost ruffled, sometimes unshaven. Personalitywise, the spectrum seems covered: Gwenn—spontaneous, earthy, transparent, an extrovert, more apparently given to insecurity and bouts with joy; John—less so, more outwardly level and internally combustible, with a fondness for pushing the edges, a subtle risk taker.

But deeper, where their lives have been lived, they share hearts broken past the point of despair, crushed and numbed by circumstances, touched deeply and unimaginably by the love and grace of God, and, with each new moment of deep dependency, healing. They both know what it means to descend, without control.

They also share possibilities: for struggles and for joy, both at the level of the seemingly impossible.

———————————

Reagan, Gwenn's fifteen-year-old daughter, is in the bathroom preparing for her mother's second wedding. She is wrestling with a fit of giggles, the hiccupy kind that teenage girls are uniquely prone to, and—when she can catch her breath—singing along with a song on the radio . . . *Give me something to believe in, something to believe in.* . . . What she thought was an unmarked bottle of hair spray turned out to be something to stop the cats from using spaces other than the litter box. Something repelling. It's cracking her up, freaking her out, turning her voice shrill. Everything at the same time . . . *Give me something to believe in. . . .* The energy, needless to say, is running high.

She seems a typical teenager.

Just two years ago, at the age of thirteen, she was the one to find her father's body. It was in the corner of the bedroom in the house where she used to live, wrapped in a blanket, shriveled, almost to the bone, inexpressibly sad. She still remembers the touch, the unexpected sensation of cold flesh, the icy tingle that spread along her nerves. It stunned her, but she was not surprised. Even at her young age, she knew her father's drinking would lead to this. In a way she was relieved: no longer would she or her family have to put up with the abuse. No longer would her father have to endure the humiliation and pain of deterioration. Still, there was the grief. As the ambulance came, she remembered her father's last words to her. Through a drunken haze, almost more of a plea than a statement: "I love you."

The song fades . . . *Give me something to believe in. . . .* Reagan has found the hair spray and, freshly recovered from a case of the giggles, her hair, as well as her composure, is once again in place.

There was a time in his life when John Tindall never thought he would see the day when he was married. In fact, just a few years ago, he never thought he would see another day. The good life had left him high and dry. Straight out of college, he became a high-powered ad executive and quickly had everything that money, or at least a credit card, could buy. He would fly to Cancun with his girlfriend on a moment's notice. He bought two new cars in less than two years. He would often knock off work for afternoons on the beach. He drank like a fish, often tanked at company expense, and had thrills out the gills.

"I thought I had everything," John says. What he ended up with was nothing. Inexplicably, the depression, which had caused him to become suicidal in college, returned. He quit his job in search of a better one (in southern California, of course), which he ended up quitting. He lost all of his money and was deeply in debt. He lost his girlfriend, whom he had gotten engaged to just to keep the relationship from disintegrating. The self-esteem issues, rooted in the separation from his family that he experienced as a child at missionary boarding schools, returned to haunt him. He drank to escape, to find release—from the pent-up emotions he had stuffed inside, and from the realities of dealing with life.

"The good times were good," John says. "But they were always too short . . . and there comes a day when the bill comes due." For John, that day came in January of 1988. In Michigan, they pay for returned cans and bottles. John had been reduced to scrounging along the roadside, looking for his next drink. His best friend was moving to Iowa and the winter was numbing cold. He decided to get in his car and drive as far toward Key West as $20 would take him. He could hitchhike the rest of the way. He wanted to be a bum. He got as far as a rest area in Indianapolis before coming to his senses. He returned home, admitted he had a drinking problem, called his parents, and asked if he could live with them. They agreed, but on one condition: that he go to church.

————————

At the Doubletake beauty salon, Gwenn Schumacher, dressed in black stretch pants, a white tumbledown short-sleeved shirt, and her wedding veil, is running out of time. It's 2:33, hours into the appointment, and her hair is not yet perfect. Normally compassionate and fun-loving, Gwenn, in the words of one of the stylists, has turned into "a fussbucket."

"I've waited a long time for this day," Gwenn says, "and I want my hair to be just right." At first, it's too puffy, then too flat, then too puffy on one side, too flat on the other, and then there are noticeable wings. "Let me know, Gwenn, when we get *something* right," one of the stylists jokes.

From the posters, perfect young people, faces crisp and tight, with hair designed to make huge statements, stare down on the scene, too old and one-dimensional for a good spanking. On a black-and-white checkered floor, as if in some big-as-life chess game, a crowd has gathered around Gwenn, the queen of the day. *Wings.* There's Reagan and Scottie, her eleven-year-old son, three hairstylists, anywhere between one to five customers, and one large man with a Harley tattoo, who keeps saying, "That's it, perfect." *Too flat.* From the required four-inch circular ceiling speakers specifically engineered to turn voices into kazoos, Whitney Houston wants to dance with somebody. *Too puffy.* The minutes are lost, succumbing to the pungency of the smells, the urgency of the voices.

The mood is not only the product of Gwenn's perfectionism, it's The Nerves. In a couple of hours, her life will change forever. It's not so much that she's frightened by the possibility of failure. What could be worse than living for sixteen years with an abusive and suicidal alcoholic? Just the opposite. There is a real potential for joy—God's gift of a second chance at life. What has she done to deserve that? Or, at the very least, how can she can keep herself from distrusting it? *Not right.*

She tightens the veil to hide the tears. Over the speakers, *Big Girls Don't Cry, They Don't Cry, Yii, Yii.* The timing, if one is to believe in miracles or a divine sense of humor, is amazing. To an unbeliever, unbelievable.

John Tindall and Gwenn Schumacher's wedding wasn't exactly made in heaven. Slightly south of there, real south. On the exterior, there were all the warning signs. Two needy people. One, a woman who lived with an alcoholic for sixteen tortuous years; the other, a recovering alcoholic. The red flags were everywhere. The red flag of co-dependency, an unhealthy alliance of two needy people clinging to one another in a desperate and ultimately self-destructive attempt to have their needs met. The red flag of unhealthy childhoods, in which both suffered from a lack of self-esteem and intimacy. The red flags of age difference, temperament difference, and a history of past addictions—John to alcohol; Gwenn to food. There were so many red flags that they nearly put the red flag business out of business. There were so many unhealthy patterns, so much excess baggage, the possibility of flight seemed like a death wish.

And then there was God. The God of the impossible. The God of the second chance. But, even that, in the face of such circumstances was not enough. According to the ministers at the church that John and Gwenn attend, the possibility of their marriage involved a union of God and faith. Both had a deep commitment to renewing their minds in biblical wisdom. They learned and applied what God had to say about parenting, relationships, God, substance abuse, conflict resolution, and many other issues. They were willing to even lay aside plans for their marriage, if necessary.

Separately, at first, and then together, John, Gwenn, and her children began taking "teachability steps" through the ministries of their church. They demonstrated a teachable spirit and a deep dependency on God as they descended into the problems of their pasts and their pain, desperation, and failures.

Says one of the pastors that worked with John and Gwenn: "They didn't get focused on what they didn't know or what the future might hold, but, rather they focused on the next step—what can we do to bring about healing in *this* particular area." As they worked through the ministries, they learned about issues such as co-dependency, repressed anger in children, learned about destructive patterns, addictions, poor self-esteem. . . . They became aware of their baggage—emotional, relational, and spiritual.

They also showed a willingness to apply God's principles, painful as they may be, to their shattered lives. There has been much progress, and there is a long way to go. John and Gwenn know there are no guarantees. They have both learned, however, that they cannot depend upon themselves for their own happiness. They must trust in God, stay submitted to Him and each other, and see what happens. Joy, if it strikes, will take them by surprise.

An hour before the wedding, Gwenn's hair is finally right, but she forgot the card with her wedding vows. She doesn't want to make them up. In front of the wall-length mirror of the bride's room, she strains her memory and mouths the words in between hugs of encouragement and tears of joy. "I can't wait to see him," she tells nearly everyone.

There is the usual hubbub that precedes the wedding: a chaotic, but easily scripted string of events: the Hey Charlie You Ole Dog Slap on the Backs, the tender smiles, the ordered confusion of musicians tuning up, the notes on sequence, who goes where and when, sound checks and photography flashes, the pictures that will eventually yellow with the years in an album of memories.

In the excitement, it is easy to feel lost in the crowd. Especially if you are eleven and your mom is getting married. Scottie is blond and quiet, tender at heart, uncomfortable in crowds and more so in front of a camera. As the wedding photographer snaps freeze-frames, Scottie is caught half-slumping, half-smiling—that awkward, gangly moment in time when boy meets young man and doesn't yet recognize himself. The tuxedo, oversized, makes the contrast stiff.

Scottie is a picture of many things: longing, grace, burned innocence, buried hurt and, to some extent, restored hope. He still misses his real father, the one that always picked on him, called him idiot, Mongoloid, worthless. The father that once threw him against a wall. When he wasn't drinking, Scottie says, there were good memories: going to the beach, flying kites, playing catch. He loved his father and hated him. Like the time Scottie was pitching in an All-Stars baseball game, and his father came drunk and hurled obscenities and insults at his son. "I tried to pretend that he wasn't my dad," Scottie says.

After his funeral, he wrote his dad a note: "Dear Dad, I'll miss you. If you ever get this I want to tell you this is what you get for taking drugs and drinking. It's kind of better that you died in the house, not on the street. I'll miss your help with my homework."

It was through Scottie that his mom met John. Scottie was in a ministry at his church, learning about anger and hurt and John was one of his teachers. Eventually, both Scottie and his mom fell in love with John. Neither one of them intended that to happen.

Once again, Scottie has hope for happiness. "The best thing about God to me is making me and Mom and John and Reagan to be a family." Hope is just *one* of the emotions that, in his quietness, surges deep. Just six weeks before the marriage, his sister was in the bathroom and, as teenage girls tend to do, overstayed her visit. Scottie wanted in. He got his baseball bat.

In the door, one hour before his mom's wedding, the hole still remains.

John and Gwenn believe in miracles. They have had, they say, first-hand experience. Their relationship with Jesus Christ and their dependency on Him to meet needs has transformed their lives, their perspectives, and their dreams. They have been given enough second chances to descend toward joy.

The list of miracles could go on and on. Both have experienced the "best" of what the world can offer, and the worst. Just a few years ago, both were, at one point or another, suicidal. Now, they cling to life. A short time ago, both were addicted—John scrounging in garbage cans looking for tin cans to buy more alcohol; Gwenn eating herself into 243 pounds of near-oblivion. Both are now healthy, stripped of the weight of yielding to compulsive behaviors. Through separation and the death of her first husband in 1988, Gwenn has been freed from abuse—the obscenities, the tire iron attacks, the nightmares of her children—and, through it, has learned how to hold an ongoing conversation with God. Both Reagan and Scottie, through their own desire to heal, are seeking help to work through repressed emotions.

The biggest miracle they have experienced, however, is the miracle of the church. The teaching of the Word of God, for sure, but even more, the people of God. Through the ministries, they have developed caring relationships that have changed their lives. Says John: "God gave us these people. They are valuable, incredible gifts in our lives." Says Gwenn, matter-of-factly: "Without the church, I don't think we would be alive."

Because of the church's ministry to them, they are now able to serve others. "That's the beauty of the body of Christ," says John. "You have people using their gifts to serve. You can take out what you need and then, when you can, you can put back what you can give. That's the whole picture—being served so that you can serve."

John and Gwenn's ministry in life, their purpose statement, has been dramatically changed. They have seen the fallacy of the world's priorities: good times, pleasure seeking, money making. They have found them bankrupt, almost murderous. Through brokenness, God has dramatically restructured their value systems. "What we have learned," John says, "is that life is all about making a difference in people's lives."

Their ministry, for the time being, is tightly focused and highly defined: creating a loving family. It is an impact, they say, that can last through eternity.

"The influence that I can have on Scottie," John says by way of example, "can continue to make a difference after I have left the planet. If I can build self-esteem into him, so that he knows that he matters, and if he can pass that on to his kids, then we have broken a destructive pattern. To me, that would be a major victory because not only can negative patterns be passed on, but so can positive ones."

Joy is a real possibility. "I used to feel like a road map," Gwenn says. Now, they say, there is direction. "Isn't joy more meaningful against a backdrop of pain? If you lived life on a permanent high, when would you know the thrill of joy?"

At the altar, John, Gwenn, Reagan, and Scottie stand, now as a family. There are tears. John, in a matter of minutes, is becoming a husband and a father. He is finishing his vows: "I thank God for the miracle of this relationship," he says. For John, Gwenn, Reagan, and Scottie, another in a series of miracles.

The pastor speaks of dependency, the music celebrates friendship, and the ceremony is over. Mr. and Mrs. John Tindall and family. The announcement of the grace of God.

———————————

The honeymoon is over. John and Gwenn, as they have known all along, are aware that the road before them is not an easy one. Already, old patterns have surfaced. Gwenn was up in the middle of the night, fighting a compulsion to eat. Scottie was demonstrating more patterns of anger. John is wrestling with feelings of rejection. Reagan has been wary of the new family arrangement, specifically the discipline, the new order.

Each time, however, the needs have been brought before God with a sense of deep dependency. Progress has happened. It will not always be that way.

It is, they know, the process that matters. "We are well aware of the needs, the baggage we bring into this marriage," says John. "But because of how big the needs are, we know that, day to day, we need a big God. We need a God that is a lot bigger and more powerful than us. It's exciting to live knowing that you need a big God."

———————————

EPILOGUE

John officially adopted the children a few months later. They are now Tindalls. Scottie was diagnosed with an Attention Deficit Disorder and, through counseling and medication, has greatly improved his attention span and his grades have improved from C's and D's to mostly A's and B's. He is excelling in track and baseball. Reagan, outgoing and likable, is a leader in her church youth group and a student athlete.

John and Gwenn remain best friends.

A CHOICE

14

TAKING THE
DOWNWARD PATH

*"Continue to work out your salvation with fear
and trembling, for it is God who works in you to
will and to act according to his good purpose."*
—*Philippians 2:12–13*

I wish, for my own self, that I had a nice, tidy definition of downward mobility. Something I could pull out
of my wallet, unfold, and hold on to. Something crisp
and black-and-white: ink on a page. Something that
told me, without any uncertainty, how to consistently
descend into God's greatness.

In my own struggle with descending, I wish
constantly for a clean definition. *Keep your salary under
$50,000. Give all your possessions away. Refuse titles of
honor. Resist fame. Hug street people.* That would make
things easier. Often, I am more than willing to descend,
but I am not sure how that plays out in my everyday
world. In fact, the deeper I get into faith and life

circumstances, the more difficulty I have distinguishing how to descend.

Several years ago, as I was preparing a series of messages on the book of Philippians, the concept of descending into greatness hit me with a force that nearly leveled me. Maybe it was its very resistance to easy definitions that struck me so. The concept refused to be reduced to a set of rules. I couldn't define it with salary figures, titles, or positions of power. Still, there seemed to be attached to it a concrete sense of intentionality. Although the idea of descending was and still is somewhat difficult to define, it clearly requires choice. Whatever it means, descending into greatness is the way of Jesus Christ. If we want to follow in the footsteps of the Son of God, we have to consciously move down.

In my mind, descending is primarily a matter of attitude: *What is most important to me? What drives my thoughts and actions? What gives me a sense of value?* Curiously, Christianity, in its purest form, is not bent on human self-fulfillment. Its overriding purpose is simple and to the point: God's kingdom come. Christians, then, are those who roll up their sleeves to advance God's kingdom. They give themselves away in love, so God and others might receive. They make decisions not on the basis of economic, social, or status factors, but with only one question in mind: Does this bring God's kingdom on earth closer to reality?

Descending, contrary to self-fulfillment, involves emptying: to push aside one's own selfish desires and pleasures, so the good of others can be considered. The Christian faith, when it works right, is more a matter of giving than receiving. That much is clear in Philippians 2 as Jesus Christ, the Son of God Himself, yields divine privileges and worship, makes Himself "nothing," becomes a servant, humbles Himself, becomes obedient, and dies on a cross. His overriding purpose: to advance the kingdom of God. It is obvious that Jesus would have flunked "Self-Fulfillment 101."

But there is in Philippians, and in life, a curious twist. Following verse 8 of chapter 2, the author states, "Therefore God exalted him to the highest place." By giving himself completely, without selfish ambition, He received everything. Christians, too, are promised joy and rewards from God when they fully commit themselves to unconditional love for others. Down—those steps away from self-indulgence and toward God and others—mysteriously becomes up.

I can relate. I know what it feels like to take giant steps down—to the point of feeling like I was free-falling into an abyss—and yet land at the pinnacle of God's grace and freedom. As a young adult, I sensed God asking me to leave the marketplace to pursue some form of vocational ministry. My decision to do that set in motion a series of decisions that involved a rapid and intense plunge. I "descended" in the sense that a man does when he jumps from a plane.

The first decision—to enter vocational ministry—was one of the more difficult decisions of my life. I had to leave our family business, a highly successful wholesale produce company in Kalamazoo, Michigan. That decision involved more than a career shift; it was a change in calling. All my life, my father had prepared me not only to assume a position of leadership in the company, but to ascend to greatness in every way. He believed in me, and looked for every opportunity to develop my potential. He delighted in throwing challenges my way. He taught me never to say "I can't." I could drive the company pickup trucks by the time I was in first grade and semi tractor-trailer rigs by sixth grade. I sailed a forty-five foot sailboat solo on Lake Michigan in seventh grade. I toured Africa and Europe for eight weeks alone when I was fifteen. My father taught me not to be afraid of the unknown, and instilled in me the value of hard work. He believed there was no end to my potential.

I believed it, too. After two years of college and the study of business theory nearly bored me to death, I returned to the family business prepared to follow in my father's footsteps. I loved the adrenaline of the marketplace. I was charged up by the challenge—to do things a little more efficiently, to organize better, to maximize resources. And to make a ton of money. I knew where I was headed and what I wanted.

And then came a leading from the Holy Spirit. The director of a Christian camp I worked at during the summers pulled me off to the side and asked me a question that shook me to my foundations. "Bill, what are you doing with your life that will last forever?" The question haunted me. I began to realize that my whole existence was wrapped around the here and now. Everything I was doing was self-centered and temporary. That question stripped me naked, and I discovered that without the planes and boats and fast cars I had little to give my life meaning. As I continued to work at the produce company, I felt more and more restless. Finally I decided I needed to serve the Lord more directly. I wanted to be on the front lines of the spiritual battle.

When I told my dad of my decision, he said, "Fine, Bill. Now turn in your credit cards and your keys to the plane, the boat, and the cars. And don't entertain any ideas of coming back."

I got a job in a shipping department of a Christian organization in the Chicagoland area. I made minimum wage. I was nineteen. I'll never forget the time my father flew in to visit me. I was standing between two middle-aged women, stuffing little plastic awards into cellophane wrappers. My dad looked at his son, for whom he had held such high hopes. Not one usually given to changing his mind, he took me to lunch and said, "You can get on that plane with me and come home." I told him no; I didn't want to miss the adventure. And I meant it!

That choice involved more than just a step down financially and a loss of toys. I moved away from home, where, through my family name, I had been recognized and respected. My network of friends, who had massaged my youthful ego, was suddenly gone. I was now just a face in the crowd, a nobody.

Then came the next step down. I decided to teach a Bible study for a group of teenagers at a church in Park Ridge, Illinois. It was part-time pay for a full-time job. I had no idea if I could teach the Bible effectively, or whether I had leadership gifts, but I poured myself into the challenge. Soon I began to realize the rewards of descending. The youth group grew from about fifty kids to over one thousand in three years. I am convinced that the results had little to do with my brilliance, or that of the other leaders. Rather, God was pleased with an attitude—a willingness to use whatever talents we had and whatever resources were available to advance His kingdom.

There is no way to describe the exhilaration we felt as we watched this youth group blossom. We saw kids sell out for the cause of Christ and start serving and loving one another. We watched hundreds of young people come to Jesus Christ as Savior and Lord. We got to observe the whole high school Pecking Order dissolve as star athletes hugged the mentally retarded or the homecoming queen sat with a pock-faced freshman. We saw teenagers gathering together to pray for the salvation of their parents. I learned what it was like to be part of the family of God.

Just about that time, two significant things happened: I got married and I received a pay raise. Lynne and I were delighted with our prospects for the future: a successful ministry, decent pay, and a sense of stability. What more could we want? Then came a new calling from the Holy Spirit to start a church. No matter how hard I tried, I could not shake it. And I did try to shake it. The idea was totally illogical. I would have to leave the youth group and the miracle we had experienced together. I would have to trade the known for the absolutely unknown. I was twenty-three; most of us who wanted to start the church didn't know anybody over thirty. We had no money, experience, people, facility, elders, location, or demographic studies . . . you get the idea. All we did have was willingness and availability, and I wasn't too sure how they would stack up against the obvious possibility of failure. Responding to this call would clearly be a new high for me in the art of descending.

Lynne and I had just bought a cracker box house and furnished it with garage sale giveaways. In order to survive for the first couple years, we took in boarders, sold possessions, and Lynne taught flute. There were times when we did not know where the next meal or mortgage payment was coming from. God used this era to strip me of my pride and a misplaced sense of values. Growing up, I had always been in a position of having, of power, and of giving. I had never had to depend on anyone for anything. I had been proud of my independence. Now things were reversed. One of my lifelong friends, Joel Jager, grew up with me in Michigan. Because there was a sizable socioeconomic gap between his family and mine, I had a decided "material edge"; in fact, my father bought Joel his first car. Secretly I liked this arrangement. But when we both moved to the Chicago area and started a new church, things changed. Joel found a high-paying job in a tool-and-die factory; he lent me money for housing and food. The descent was painful at first, but it taught me in unforgettable language about the beauty and benefit of interdependence, humility, and love.

We started the church in a rented movie theater in 1975. Within a year, a thousand people were attending each Sunday. By 1978 that number had doubled. We were bursting at the seams at all three of our morning services, so we decided to buy land and build a facility. We had made ourselves available, and God was using us; we had to pinch ourselves to make sure we weren't dreaming.

I did not realize I was about to experience a new form of descending. This step down felt like the bottom dropping out. Without knowing it, some of us young, zealous leaders had become addicted to ministry. Every day we were seeing lives transformed and the course of eternity changed. Hundreds and hundreds of people were coming to know Christ and finding their place in a true community of fellowship and support. There was an electricity and a love. God was working in extraordinary ways.

And the more He worked, the more difficult it became for us to pull away. In an effort to see more fruit borne, we put in longer and longer hours. *If we worked seventy hours a week and touched this many lives, we reasoned, what would happen if we worked eighty hours, or ninety?* We neglected our families, our health, and each other. There was no real structure for accountability. The pace soon overwhelmed us; cracks began to appear in the foundation—fatigue, relational carelessness, sin. One of the cofounders of the church left and was divorced within a year. With his departure, others in the church core departed. Where there once was love and trust, there was now increasing fear and suspicion. To make matters worse, we were in the midst of a major fund-raising program for a facility already under construction.

Circumstances began to collapse in on me. Within a year, my father died, and the person whose belief in me had shaped me was gone. My wife miscarried. My marriage began to disintegrate from the effects of my workaholism. My best friend and cofounder of the church had left. The staff was burning out, and the core was splitting. I blamed myself for the brokenness. In the midst of the pain, I spent an entire night face down on our living room floor pleading for forgiveness, for one more chance. This time there would be no compromises; we would do it God's way. It is difficult to describe how far I descended that night. It was my Gethsemane prayer. There was, at the same time, excruciating pain and calming release. I gave it to God, and was content to leave the results to Him. In a room filled with hand-me-down furniture, I experienced anew the richness of God's grace.

Slowly things began to fall into place. Through supernatural intervention, the church recovered, funding came in for the building, accountable relationships were established, and Willow Creek is flourishing today. I also recovered and began to establish a better balance in my personal life. I rebuilt my marriage and made my kids a priority. My external circumstances also began to improve. Today I live in a comfortable house, and I no longer have to wonder where the mortgage and food money will come from. Life is not nearly as complicated as it used to be.

Externally, anyway. Internally, where my faith rubs against reality, it's another story. There, life seems more complicated than ever. Descending has become an option, and with the option come new pressures.

In my early years of ministry, when Lynne and I earned less than enough to pay our own living expenses, we didn't have to make decisions about moving down. Responding to God's call on our lives *required* descending. Starting a church with no money, no people, and no building made the descent inevitable. We lived on little because we had to. We tithed whatever excess we had because the church needed it, and served because there was so much to do and so few to do it. To some extent, we moved down on auto-pilot.

That doesn't mean descending was easy. God used those years, I believe, to strip me of my dependence on everyone and everything that was not God. First He took the things of pleasure, the machines and toys of my youth. Then He broke my independent spirit, or more simply, my pride. He forced me to be so needy that I *had* to see the beauty of the loving help of the family of God. There were periods when He shut down the accolades of others, and I had only His whisper of approval to hang on to. He made me face losing it all and possibly the sight of my ministry crumbling in front of my eyes. Consistently and powerfully, God led me on the path down, so He could tear away every barbed hook in my life that kept me from being an effective servant.

Now externally many would consider me "successful." Willow Creek is visible across the nation and world. I make a decent salary and have written some books. Some people might cite the recent upward trajectory of my life as evidence that I lack the credibility to author a book about moving down. And perhaps they are right. If our descent into God's greatness can be measured accurately by how few digits decorate our paycheck or how lowly is our title at work or how obscure we are to the public, then I would have to agree. But is that basic assumption correct? Are paychecks and titles and recognition—or the lack thereof—the true measures of one's heart?

The real-life stories in this book suggest otherwise. In previous chapters, you have read of people from various backgrounds, professions, demographics, and economic classes. They share little but a desire to determine in their own lives what it means to descend for the advancement of the kingdom of God. For each one, the path is different, based on the Holy Spirit's specific guidance to them. None of them has sighted, much less reached, the bottom rung. It is always a struggle, mixed along the way with surprising splashes of joy.

In this particular stage of my life, my descent has become complicated by options. Few of the paths that lie before me now actually go down of their own accord. Responding to God's ministry call on my life now seldom makes the same financial and lifestyle demands it used to. I now have to make conscious choices to descend. Five years ago I chose to freeze my salary from Willow Creek. This was, in part, to protect the church from media reports that the senior pastor was making a six-figure salary. But even more importantly, I did't want to facilitate a lifestyle of constant "ascent" in my own life. In our giving, whether to our church or to individuals in need, Lynne and I earnestly try to respond generously to the leadings we receive from the Holy Spirit. We have been blessed to help the poor in various parts of the world and privileged to help pay for the education of some who can't get professional training for ministry.

I mention these choices not to draw attention to our giving—we have never given anything in heroic fashion or in a way worthy of honor—but to highlight the struggle. Daily I battle the questions. Am I a traitor to Philippians 2 for no longer giving all my excess income to the church the way I did ten years ago? Is it wrong to set aside college funds for my children? Would a particularly needy person be better served by my financial assistance or by facing the consequences of irresponsible behavior?

Success not only necessitates tough decisions about how to use our money; it also makes us work harder to maintain proper attitudes. Today Lynne and I can start new ministries, give new messages, write new books—without the requirements made by downward mobility. In fact, we are generously rewarded for our efforts. But it's a reward that hides a whole new set of hooks. With the attention and the affluence comes the temptation to "think more highly of ourselves than we ought to think." The more time we spend with people of influence, the easier it is to get lured into the entrapments of power. Being with the "haves" can make it hard to remember the needs of the "have-nots."

There was a time when I seriously thought of removing myself from the spotlight, of trying to backtrack to the time when downward mobility was less a matter of choice than necessity. But that, I believe, reflected an improper understanding of descending. It made positions, titles, and salaries antonyms of moving down. In reality, the issue is not so much about how *much* power you have, but about how you *use* the power you have. It is not about the size of the check you take to the bank, but what you do with the check once you deposit it. The question is: How do you manage who you are and what has been given to you, whether that be money, authority, talent, or influence? The answer to that question will be determined, even through the shades of gray, by your central purpose in life. Whose agenda do you want to advance? Yours or God's?

Power, money, and talent. If we expend them on ourselves, we can spit-polish our external reality. But it is only when we use our resources for God's service that we experience an inward glow. And there is a world of difference between the two shines. What is important for each one of us is to maintain an attitude of willingness, yieldedness, obedience, and availability for God's call.

This is, at the same time, both more difficult and much easier than it seems. On the one hand, without a black-and-white definition, things tend to get muddy. The path down is littered with ambiguities. On the other hand, we often make the question bigger than it needs to be. I have found that the real fight for downward mobility is fought on the battlefield of the day-to-day "small" decisions. These tiny tugs of the Holy Spirit are easy to ignore or, if we are out of communion with God, not even notice. But they are the stepping stones that form the downward path.

For example, I was at the airport not long ago. It was busy and I was in a hurry. Flights had been canceled and I was standing in a long line of people waiting for a limited number of seats. Everything was chaos; anger and profanity were exploding like geysers around the terminal. I remember glancing at my watch, calculating the minutes left before my flight, and then spotting them: an eighty-year-old man and woman who were desperately trying to get out of everyone's way. The man couldn't even lift his suitcase. He was trying with his wife's help to drag it along. Both of them were bumping into people frantically moving in the other direction. They looked like animals blinded by headlights, their eyes filled with fear. At that point,

I felt the tug of the Holy Spirit and the urging to go help them. I looked at my watch again. I would miss my plane.

The choice I had to make had nothing to do with power or money or title or talent or influence. It was about being available and willing to respond to God's call. The Holy Spirit's request was that I help this elderly couple with their suitcase and flight arrangements, and the One making the request expected obedience. Had He asked me to charter the couple an airplane, He would have expected the same obedience. Downward mobility isn't a matter of what the Holy Spirit asks of me, but whether or not I respond to what He asks.

The choices I make on this downward path are up to me. Sometimes I disobey the Spirit's leading, choose for self, and pay the price of emptiness and disappointment. Sometimes I take a headlong plunge for others and nearly burst with fulfillment and joy.

The same choices exist for you, the choices that will mark your journey down. I can't tell you how to choose any more than you can tell me how to choose. But I can tell you there is high adventure on the downward path. And the destination is greatness in God's eyes.